COMBATING THE EBOLA THREAT

HEARING

BEFORE THE

SUBCOMMITTEE ON AFRICA, GLOBAL HEALTH, GLOBAL HUMAN RIGHTS, AND INTERNATIONAL ORGANIZATIONS

OF THE

COMMITTEE ON FOREIGN AFFAIRS HOUSE OF REPRESENTATIVES

ONE HUNDRED THIRTEENTH CONGRESS

SECOND SESSION

AUGUST 7, 2014

Serial No. 113–209

Printed for the use of the Committee on Foreign Affairs

Available via the World Wide Web: http://www.foreignaffairs.house.gov/ or http://www.gpo.gov/fdsys/

U.S. GOVERNMENT PRINTING OFFICE

89–385PDF   WASHINGTON : 2014

For sale by the Superintendent of Documents, U.S. Government Printing Office
Internet: bookstore.gpo.gov   Phone: toll free (866) 512–1800; DC area (202) 512–1800
Fax: (202) 512–2104   Mail: Stop IDCC, Washington, DC 20402–0001

COMMITTEE ON FOREIGN AFFAIRS

EDWARD R. ROYCE, California, *Chairman*

CHRISTOPHER H. SMITH, New Jersey
ILEANA ROS-LEHTINEN, Florida
DANA ROHRABACHER, California
STEVE CHABOT, Ohio
JOE WILSON, South Carolina
MICHAEL T. McCAUL, Texas
TED POE, Texas
MATT SALMON, Arizona
TOM MARINO, Pennsylvania
JEFF DUNCAN, South Carolina
ADAM KINZINGER, Illinois
MO BROOKS, Alabama
TOM COTTON, Arkansas
PAUL COOK, California
GEORGE HOLDING, North Carolina
RANDY K. WEBER SR., Texas
SCOTT PERRY, Pennsylvania
STEVE STOCKMAN, Texas
RON DeSANTIS, Florida
DOUG COLLINS, Georgia
MARK MEADOWS, North Carolina
TED S. YOHO, Florida
SEAN DUFFY, Wisconsin
CURT CLAWSON, Florida

ELIOT L. ENGEL, New York
ENI F.H. FALEOMAVAEGA, American
    Samoa
BRAD SHERMAN, California
GREGORY W. MEEKS, New York
ALBIO SIRES, New Jersey
GERALD E. CONNOLLY, Virginia
THEODORE E. DEUTCH, Florida
BRIAN HIGGINS, New York
KAREN BASS, California
WILLIAM KEATING, Massachusetts
DAVID CICILLINE, Rhode Island
ALAN GRAYSON, Florida
JUAN VARGAS, California
BRADLEY S. SCHNEIDER, Illinois
JOSEPH P. KENNEDY III, Massachusetts
AMI BERA, California
ALAN S. LOWENTHAL, California
GRACE MENG, New York
LOIS FRANKEL, Florida
TULSI GABBARD, Hawaii
JOAQUIN CASTRO, Texas

AMY PORTER, *Chief of Staff*   THOMAS SHEEHY, *Staff Director*
JASON STEINBAUM, *Democratic Staff Director*

———

SUBCOMMITTEE ON AFRICA, GLOBAL HEALTH, GLOBAL HUMAN RIGHTS, AND INTERNATIONAL ORGANIZATIONS

CHRISTOPHER H. SMITH, New Jersey, *Chairman*

TOM MARINO, Pennsylvania
RANDY K. WEBER SR., Texas
STEVE STOCKMAN, Texas
MARK MEADOWS, North Carolina

KAREN BASS, California
DAVID CICILLINE, Rhode Island
AMI BERA, California

(II)

CONTENTS

COMBATING THE EBOLA THREAT

THURSDAY, AUGUST 7, 2014

House of Representatives,
Subcommittee on Africa, Global Health,
Global Human Rights, and International Organizations,
Committee on Foreign Affairs,
Washington, DC.

The subcommittee met, pursuant to notice, at 2 o'clock p.m., in room 2172, Rayburn House Office Building, Hon. Christopher H. Smith (chairman of the subcommittee) presiding.

Mr. SMITH. The subcommittee will come to order, and good afternoon to everyone.

I have called this emergency hearing today during recess to address a grave and serious health threat which has in recent weeks gripped the mass media and heightened public fears of an epidemic, the Ebola virus. What we hope to gain from today's hearing is a realistic understanding of what we are up against while avoiding sensationalism.

Ebola is a severe, often fatal disease that first emerged or was discovered in 1976 and has killed 90 percent of its victims in some past outbreaks. Since March of this year there have been more than 1,700 cases of Ebola, including more than 900 fatalities in Guinea, Liberia, Sierra Leone, and Nigeria. This time, the average fatality rate in this outbreak is estimated at 55 percent, ranging from 74 percent in Guinea to 42 percent in Sierra Leone. The disparity in mortality rates is partially linked to the capacity of governments to treat and contain the disease and per capita health spending by affected governments.

There is also concern that given modern air travel and the latency time of the disease, the virus will jump borders and threaten lives elsewhere in Africa and even here in the United States. In my own State of New Jersey, at CentraState Hospital in Freehold, just a few hundred yards from my district office, precautions were taken. A person who had traveled from west Africa began manifesting symptoms, including a high fever. He was put in isolation. Thankfully, it was not Ebola, and the patient has been released.

New Jersey Health Commissioner Mary O'Dowd reiterated to me yesterday that New Jersey hospitals have infection control programs in which they train and are ready to deal with potentially infectious patients that come through their doors. She also told me that physicians and hospital workers follow very specific protocols prescribed by the CDC on how to protect themselves, as well as other patients, and how to observe a patient if they have any concerns, which includes protocols like managing a patient in isolation so that they are not around others who are not appropriately protected.

The commissioner also underscored that the Federal Government has U.S. quarantine stations throughout the country to limit introduction of any disease that might come into the United States at ports of entry like New Jersey's Newark Liberty International Airport.

I also hope our distinguished witnesses today will confirm whether sufficient resources are available and are being properly deployed to assist victims and contain the Ebola disease. Are there gaps in law and policy that Congress needs to address? To the government witnesses especially, my pledge to you is that, if legislation is needed, I will work, and I know I will be joined by colleagues on both sides of the aisle, with you to write those new policies.

As you know, key symptoms of Ebola include fever, weakness, head, joint, muscle, throat, and stomach ache, and then vomiting and diarrhea, rashes and bleeding. These symptoms are also seen in other diseases besides Ebola, which make an accurate diagnosis early on uncertain.

Earlier today I had a full briefing, a lengthy briefing with the deputy chief of staff of the President of Guinea, President Conde, Ibrahima Khalil Kaba, who said that the virus has masked many other diseases, including Lassa fever, so many of the doctors, especially those who have never seen Ebola in this part of the world before, it has been in other parts of Africa, but not in west Africa, just simply didn't think this would be Ebola. Many of them have died.

Ebola punches holes in blood vessels by breaking down the vessel walls, causing massive bleeding and shock. The virus spreads quickly, before most people's bodies can fight the infection effectively, breaking down the development of antibodies. As a result, there is massive bleeding within 7 to 10 days after infection that too often results in the death of the affected person.

Fruit bats are suspected of being a primary transmitter of Ebola to humans in west Africa. The virus is transmitted to humans through close contact with the blood, secretions, organs, or other bodily fluids of infected animals. Some health workers, such as the heroic American missionary aid workers, Dr. Kent Brantly and nursing assistant Nancy Writebol, had contracted the disease despite taking every precaution while helping Ebola patients. Both of them are now being treated at Emory Hospital in Atlanta, Georgia, in an isolation unit after being flown to the U.S. in a specially equipped air ambulance.

While there is no known cure for Ebola, both Dr. Brantly and Ms. Writebol have been given doses of an experimental antiviral drug cocktail called ZMapp developed by a San Diego company called MAP Biopharmaceutical. They are reportedly both feeling stronger after receiving the drug, but it is considered too early to tell whether the drug itself caused improvement in their conditions.

MAP Biopharmaceutical has been working with the National Institutes of Health and the Defense Threat Reduction Agency, an arm of the military responsible for countering weapons of mass destruction, to develop an Ebola treatment for several years. The drug, which attaches to the virus cells, much like antibodies their compromised immune systems would have produced, has never been tested on humans before Dr. Brantly and Ms. Writebol, who gave their consent to be the first human trials.

There will be hope, great hope if ZMapp works in the two Americans who bravely agreed to test it and it has a positive effect. Still, it won't mean that it will be produced in great quantities quickly and sent to affected people in west Africa. It is still an experimental drug. Those who use it might be given complete information on its use again, but that still is something that our experts I hope will address.

There is also promising research being done by Tekmira Pharmaceuticals. They have come up with a drug, a process, and one of the comments that has been made, that it has never been tested on humans, that it has provided 100 percent protection from an otherwise lethal dose of Zaire ebolavirus, but again not in humans, it has been done in others, nonhumans.

Unfortunately, there are other issues that impact the ability of the international community to assist the affected governments in meeting this grave health challenge. Some of the leading doctors in their countries have died treating Ebola victims. The nongovernmental and medical personnel who are there say they are besieged not only because they are among the only medical personnel treating this exponentially spreading disease, but also because they are under suspicion by some people in these countries who are unfamiliar with this disease and they fear that doctors who treat the disease may have brought it with them. Of course, it is not true, but again myths do abound.

The current west African outbreak, as we all know and as Dr. Frieden has said, is unprecedented. Many people are not cooperating with efforts to contain the disease. There is an information gap. Despite the efforts through cell phones and radio to get the message out, of course there is still a learning curve.

As we consider what to do to meet this health challenge, I do suggest we reconsider the funding levels for pandemic preparedness, and this message is to us in Congress and to the executive branch. In the restricted budget environment in which our Government operates, funding to meet these pandemics has fallen from $201 million in Fiscal Year 2010 to an estimated $72 million in 2014. The proposed budget for Fiscal Year 2015 is $50 million, and we mustn't shortchange vital efforts to save the lives of people in these developing countries.

Dr. Tom Frieden, one of today's expert witnesses, has tried to assure the American public that our Government is doing what we can do to address the Ebola crisis. He has announced the dispatch of at least 50, perhaps more, public health experts to the region within the next 30 days. USAID, WHO, the World Bank, the British Development Agency, African Development Bank, and many others are also joining in and trying to meet this crisis.

To those who say we have no plan, I would say that planning is definitely underway, and it is being done so very aggressively. Still, there is much more that needs to be done.

I would just say finally, I have introduced legislation that is known as the End Neglected Tropical Diseases Act, which establishes the policy of the U.S. to support a broad range of implementation of research and development activities to achieve cost-effective and sustainable treatment control and, where possible, elimination of the neglected tropical diseases.

Ebola is not on WHO's list of the top 17 neglected tropical diseases, but it does fit the definition of an infection caused by pathogens that disproportionately impact individuals living in extreme poverty, especially in developing countries. Ebola had been thought to be limited to isolated areas where it could be contained. We now know that is no longer true. We need to take seriously the effort to devise more effective means of addressing this and all neglected tropical diseases.

I now yield to my good friend and colleague, the ranking member, Ms. Bass.

Ms. BASS. Mr. Chairman, thank you for your leadership and for calling today's emergency hearing to give us an opportunity to learn about and work to address the current Ebola outbreak in west Africa. I look forward to hearing directly from our witnesses today on the work their agencies and organizations are doing to combat the deadly outbreak and how they have coordinated with the governments of impacted countries. I appreciate their efforts and outreach to keep Congress informed on this ever-evolving and devastating situation.

This outbreak comes as nearly 50 African heads of state join us here in Washington, DC, this week as part of the first in history U.S.-Africa Leaders Summit. I have been honored to join my African and American colleagues as we have worked together to reach the full capacity and promise of the African continent. We have had several productive sessions that further cemented the relationship between the U.S. and African nations and highlighted areas of opportunity for us to continue to work together.

Despite the meaningful dialogue and collaboration that occurred this week, there is still work to be done. The development of healthcare capacity and global health security is just one area of collaboration for the U.S. and African nations. I do have to say that I was a little dismayed that with all of the activities that happened this week around the summit, obviously the crisis we are dealing with today is very, very important, but when it came to coverage on Africa, the coverage centered pretty much solely around Ebola.

I want to commend the steps being taken by the Governments of Liberia, Sierra Leone, Guinea, Nigeria, and the U.S., and the great work of the many health professionals from throughout the world who are doing everything they can to help people who have contracted this awful disease. With over 1,700 suspected and confirmed cases and over 900 deaths since March, the current Ebola outbreak we know is the longest lasting, widestspread, and deadliest outbreak ever recorded. This is also the first Ebola outbreak ever in west Africa and the first outbreak to be spreading in both rural areas and capital cities.

The unique nature of this outbreak has made combating the disease particularly difficult. West Africa has not faced this disease before, and communities, government, and health professionals in the nations do not have the expertise and capacity to address the scale, spread, and proper treatment of the Ebola outbreak.

This lack of logistical expertise, healthcare workforce, and supplies has hindered the ability of governments to quickly identify, track, and isolate new cases and properly care for those infected. Officials have also had to fight against fear of the disease and cultural unfamiliarity with proper treatment, which have really contributed to the spread and kept people from seeking care.

Yesterday, I had the privilege to speak to President Ellen Johnson Sirleaf on the impact of the outbreak on her country and the work they have done to fight the disease. I asked her what more we could be doing, and one of the things she talked about was the need for logistical support, the need for training of their healthcare workforce so that they would know how to prevent the disease. I am sure Dr. Frieden, and I spoke with him yesterday, also is going to say that we do know how to prevent the spread of the disease, but that is where our efforts need to be directed.

The other thing that the President said was that the problem, of course, with the outbreak is all of the resources are centered toward the outbreak, and then just routine medical care has really suffered because there hasn't been the workforce to be able to handle both.

So President Sirleaf called for increased international assistance to provide food and water to impacted communities. She said that the communities that were most heavily impacted were quarantined and that there needed to be food and water brought into the areas. Especially in situations like this you have a concern that civil unrest could be an outbreak, especially in areas that are quarantined that feel that they do not have access. And so she felt that that was one of the ways that the United States could help the best.

It is obviously in our interest and in the world's interest to assist in the crisis and to continue to support nations as they fight this outbreak and work to develop and strengthen their healthcare systems. Healthcare is a human right, and we must ensure that countries have the ability to address this outbreak and we are able to move forward and prevent future health epidemics from occurring.

Both the chairman and I have introduced legislation to respond to this crisis, and I look forward to your testimonies, and I am interested in hearing from all of you about what more Congress can do to assist your efforts to combat the disease outbreaks and support international efforts to improve healthcare systems around the world.

Thank you.

Mr. SMITH. Thank you very much, Ms. Bass.

I would just like to recognize in the audience, Zainab Bangura, who is the Special Representative to the Secretary General of the U.N. on Sexual Violence in Conflict. Thank you for joining us today.

I would like to now yield to the distinguished chairman of the Commerce, Justice, Science, and Related Agencies Subcommittee of the Appropriations Committee, Congressman Frank Wolf, who has had a 34-year career of tremendous support for the weakest and the most vulnerable. As a matter of fact, the genesis of this hearing was a conversation with Ken Isaacs from Samaritan's Purse last week. We were planning on a hearing on the Ebola virus for September, and the sense of urgency—and Chairman Wolf was the one who set up that conference call—the sense of urgency was so great that the thought was that it is better now, and we can have more hearings in the future and more action plans and the like. So I want to thank the chairman for his tireless efforts on behalf of the weak and vulnerable.

Chairman Wolf.

Mr. WOLF. Thank you, Mr. Smith.

I want to thank my good friend Chairman Chris Smith for pulling together today's hearings on such a short notice amid the escalating outbreak of Ebola across west Africa countries, including Liberia, Sierra Leone, Guinea, and now Nigeria. I also appreciate him inviting me to join today's hearing. Although not a member of the Foreign Affairs Committee, I do serve on the State and Foreign Operations Appropriations Subcommittee, which funds the State Department and foreign aid programs.

I would also say to the witnesses, too, if you need extra money, you ought to ask for reprogramming. You ought not to be waiting until September, October, November, and December. You should ask for it immediately, and I am confident that the appropriate committees up here will allow it. But if in doubt, there should be the request for the reprogramming.

The current Ebola epidemic has claimed over 900 people since it was first detected earlier this year. It has proven to be the world's worst outbreak of the virus ever recorded. It now appears that this alarming contagious disease could be on the verge of spreading.

On July 28, I received a call from Ken Isaacs with Samaritan's Purse, one of the witnesses here today. Let me say, Samaritan's Purse and Doctors Without Borders have done more to help the poor and the suffering in many places than almost any other groups around, so I want to commend Samaritan's Purse, and I also want to commend Doctors Without Borders. Wherever you will go in Africa, they will be there when other groups have long, long gone.

Samaritan's Purse was on the front line working to curtail the Ebola outbreak. The outlook, absent immediate action from the United States, was bleak. It appears that both the international health organizations and the Obama administration underestimated the magnitude and the scope of the epidemic. Despite well-intentioned efforts by local and international aid workers, doctors and nurses working on the ground, it seems the international community and the U.S. had been noticeably absent in helping these west African countries to get out in front of the spread of this epidemic. For the first part of the epidemic, the international community simply let three of the most impoverished countries in the world deal with the Ebola threat essentially on their own. It should be no surprise that the health systems in Liberia, Guinea, and Sierra Leone do not have the resources or the capacity to deal with this epidemic on their own.

Despite early warnings from those NGOs working on the ground, there was little action taken to get out in front of this problem, and now we are seeing the consequences. Nothing can bring back the lives that were lost, and even the money and personnel deployed to help may not be enough to contain the epidemic.

I spent much of last Monday, on July 28, on the phone with the White House, State Department, CDC, and HHS trying to understand just what, if anything, the U.S. was doing both to help contain the outbreak in west Africa and prevent the spread of Ebola to the U.S. I was concerned that no one could tell me who was in charge within the administration on this issue, and no one could explain what actions are being taken to ensure the U.S. was prepared to respond. Although more progress has been made over the last week since these conversations, it is clear that the government is still trying to catch up.

This grave situation requires immediate and coordinated efforts across agencies and countries. France, Great Britain, and many of the countries in Europe who are very experienced in Africa should also be brought in.

It also has come to my attention there needs to be an immediate response to the existing deficiencies in CDC planning, procedures, and protocols in response to the Ebola threat. As Mr. Isaacs will share today, and I have read his testimony, when its two healthcare workers were confirmed with Ebola, Samaritan's Purse struggled to get guidance on protocols for dealing with returning healthcare workers from the region. It soon became apparent that there were significant gaps in existing procedures for dealing with this. The CDC had no available registry of medical facilities capable of treating Ebola patients in the United States. There are no quarantines or travel restrictions in place. And there was concern about these gaps in the protocols and how you deal with them.

I appreciate very much, and I want to thank Dr. Frieden, for taking the call, as he was getting on an airplane. I want to publicly thank you, Doctor, I am very appreciative that you are here today and hope you will talk about any deficiencies and how they can be addressed by the government and also by the Congress.

In closing, I want to thank again Chairman Smith for calling this hearing during the August recess. I also want to recognize the men and women of the CDC and other international response groups who are on the ground and will soon be on the ground in Africa, as well as the doctors and nurses helping the two patients in Atlanta. I want to thank them because this is very dangerous, what they will be doing, and what people who we do not know their names will be doing. I think we should tell them that we are appreciative.

I also want to thank the State Department and the Department of Defense for their invaluable assistance as this situation has taken place. This is important and serious work, and I know the American people, if they knew what these folks were doing and had been done, would appreciate their tireless efforts.

This should be a very top priority of the White House, the political leadership of the Nation. We know the career people, what they are going to do, but of the White House because the American people deserve to know what their government leadership is doing to prevent the spread of this epidemic and keep the country safe.

With that, Mr. Chairman, I again thank you and yield back.

Mr. SMITH. Chairman Wolf, thank you so very much.

I would like to now introduce our first panel of two panels, beginning first with Dr. Tom Frieden, who has been Director of the Centers for Disease Control and Prevention, CDC, since June 2009, and has worked to control infectious and chronic diseases in the United States and globally. He led New York City's program that controlled tuberculosis and reduced multidrug resistance cases by 80 percent and worked in India for 5 years, helping to build a tuberculosis control program that has saved nearly 3 million lives. As the commissioner of New York City's Health Department, Dr. Frieden led programs that reduced illness and death and increased life expectancy substantially. He is the recipient of numerous awards and honors and has published more than 200 scientific articles and has previously testified before this subcommittee on drug-resistant diseases, as well as other very important health topics.

Thank you, Doctor, for being here.

I then would like to introduce Dr. Ariel Pablos-Méndez, who is the Assistant Administrator for Global Health at USAID, a position he assumed in August 2011. Dr. Pablos-Méndez joined USAID's leadership team with a vision to shape the Bureau for Global Health's programmatic efforts to accomplish scaleable, sustainable, and measurable impact on the lives of people living in developing countries. Prior to joining USAID, he worked on global health strategy and transformation of health systems in Africa and Asia. He also served as Director of Knowledge Management at the World Health Organization. Dr. Pablos-Méndez is a board-certified internist and until recently was practicing as a professor of clinical medicine and epidemiology at Columbia University.

And then we will hear from Ambassador Bisa Williams, a career member of the Senior Foreign Service with the rank of Minister Counselor and currently Deputy Assistant Secretary in the Bureau of African Affairs at the U.S. Department of State. Ambassador Williams has served as Ambassador to the Republic of Niger from 2010 to 2013. She has also served in U.S. Embassies in Mauritius, France, Panama, and Guinea. Ambassador Williams' postings have also included Director for International Organizations in the National Security Council at the White House and adviser at the U.S. Mission to the United Nations in New York.

Dr. Frieden, the floor is yours.

STATEMENT OF TOM FRIEDEN, M.D., DIRECTOR, CENTERS FOR DISEASE CONTROL AND PREVENTION

Dr. FRIEDEN. Thank you so much, Chairman Smith, Ranking Member Bass, Congressman Wolf, for your interest in global health, for your interest in Ebola, and for calling this hearing at this really critical and pivotal time.

I think, first, let's remember the lives and the faces of the men, women, and children who are affected by the Ebola outbreaks in the four countries currently affected, especially the healthcare workers, who account for a substantial proportion of cases. Those are the people who we must focus on, those are the people who we must support, and it is in Africa that we can stop this outbreak and protect not only these countries, but ourselves as well.

We focus on what works, and I am incredibly proud of the staff of the Centers for Disease Control and Prevention, and I think every American who would know the expertise, dedication of the disease detectives, laboratory experts, disease intervention specialists who have been on the ground in the past few weeks and months and who are now surging for our response would be proud to know what we are doing there.

I want to start with the bottom line, three basic facts. First, we can stop Ebola. We know how to do it. It will be a long and hard fight, and the situation in Lagos, Nigeria, is particularly concerning, but we can stop Ebola. Second, we have to stop it at the source in Africa. That is the only way to get control. And, third, that we have to stop it at the source through tried and true means, the core public health interventions that work and that I will go through in a few moments.

By way of background, Ebola is one of several viral hemorrhagic fevers. There are others, but Ebola is the most feared in part because it had a movie made about it. There are others that are just as deadly. The first Ebola virus was identified in 1976 in what is now the Democratic Republic of the Congo, and there have been sporadic outbreaks since. The natural reservoir is not known but is believed to possibly be bats, which then pass it to primates and other forest-living mammals, and humans may come in contact with them by eating bush meat or contact with bats. That is a theory, there is increasing evidence for it, but we are not certain of it.

What we are certain of is that when Ebola gets into human populations it spreads by two routes. First, to people who are giving care to individuals who are sick with Ebola. Ebola does not spread from people who have been infected but are not yet sick. So it is only the sick people who transmit it. And, second, it is transmitted only by close contact with exchange of body fluid, so a healthcare worker or a family caregiver who comes into contact with a patient who is very ill, may be bleeding or have other body fluids that get on to that individual.

That is how Ebola spreads, and in the outbreaks in Africa there have been two main drivers: Healthcare settings and other caregiving settings, including the family, and burial practices, where there may be practices that involve contact with a recently deceased person. Those are the drivers of Ebola in Africa.

Again, Ebola only spreads from people who are sick and only spreads through contact with infectious body fluids. It does not spread through casual contact, it is not an airborne disease that it spreads in nature, doesn't spread through water or food, and the incubation period is usually between 8 and 10 days from exposure to onset of illness. It can be possibly as short as 2 days and possibly as long as 21 days, but in that period it is essential that any contact be very closely monitored to determine if they have developed the symptoms of Ebola, and if they have, are followed up.

We do know how to stop Ebola: Meticulous case finding; isolation; and contact tracing and management. We, with our partners, have been able to stop every Ebola outbreak to date, and I am confident that if we do what works, we will stop this one also, but it won't be quick and it won't be easy. It requires meticulous attention to detail, because if you leave behind even a single burning ember, it is like a forest fire, it flares back up. One patient not isolated, one patient not diagnosed, one healthcare worker not protected, one contact not traced, each of those lapses can result in another chain of transmission and another flare of the outbreak.

To control the outbreak, we have to work effectively. The challenge really isn't the strategy. The challenge is the implementation of that strategy. Mr. Chairman, we have provided to the committee this basic information on how Ebola can be controlled, and if you would permit me, I will just go very quickly through this because I think it is important to get the fundamentals out there.

First, to find patients and diagnose them. That means fever or other symptoms. The only way to diagnose Ebola is with a laboratory test. That is generally done by a blood test in Africa, and we, working with partners from the Department of Defense, from the Pasteur Institute of France, from other countries, and the countries where the disease is present, are scaling up the ability to diagnose patients. So the first, that diagnosis, is suspect it with fever, test with blood, get it tested in the lab. That is a critical first step.

The second step is to respond to those individual cases. We do that by putting patients in isolation, by interviewing them and eliciting their contacts, and then by following each and every contact every day for 21 days, and if a contact develops fever, begin that process all over again, interview them, isolate them, find out who their contacts are. It is laborious, it is hard, it requires local knowledge and local action, but it is how Ebola is stopped.

And, third, prevent it. Prevent it through infection control in health care, safe burial practices, and reducing the consumption or unsafe consumption of bush meat and contact with bats.

The current outbreak is a crisis. It is unprecedented, and it is unprecedented in five different ways. First, it is the largest outbreak ever. In fact, at the current trend within another few weeks there will have been more cases in this outbreak than in all previous recognized outbreaks of Ebola put together.

Second, it is multicountry, and one of the biggest challenges is that one of the epicenters is on the confluence of three different countries. And cases have moved between countries. One country gets control and then patients come in from another country, so that tricountry area is a critical challenge.

Third, this is the first outbreak in west Africa. This was a disease that was unknown, as far as we know, in that area before, and because of this, it has been a particular challenge, and the health systems in these countries are quite weak, and this also is a challenge.

Fourth, many of the cases have been in urban areas, and there has been spread in urban areas, and this is something we have not seen to this extent before. From everything we know to date, this doesn't appear to be a change in the virus, but it is a new development in how and where the virus is spreading, and it makes control much more difficult.

And, fifth, it is the first time we are having to deal with it here in the United States, and that is not merely because of the two people who became ill caring for Ebola patients and were brought back to the U.S. by their organization. That is primarily because we are all connected, and inevitably there will be travelers, American citizens and others, who go from these three countries, or from

Lagos, if it doesn't get it under control, and are here with symptoms. Those symptoms might be Ebola or something else. So we are having to deal with Ebola in the U.S. in a way that we have never had to deal with it before.

The U.S. is working in a coordinated way to support partner governments and the World Health Organization. I have activated the CDC Emergency Operations Center at Level 1 for this outbreak. This is our highest level of response. It doesn't mean that there is an increased risk to Americans, but it does mean that we are taking an extensive effort to do everything we can to stop the outbreaks.

We can't do it alone. There are many partners throughout the U.S. Government who we are working with. The World Health Organization, the World Bank, partner governments around the world, as well as, most importantly, people in-country will be key to stopping the outbreak.

We will send, as I have said, at least 50 staff to the region. Within the next week or two actually we will have reached that 50 number. But I think it is important to understand that the 50 in-country are supported at our home base in Atlanta by a much larger group. As of today, even before the full surge in activation, we have more than 200 staff working on this outbreak response, and we will increase that number substantially in the coming days and weeks.

You will hear more about the work we are doing with the U.S. Agency for International Development, where we are using an unprecedented model to work together in a collaborative way to rapidly identify and call in for reinforcements and assistance. When we finish this response, we are determined to not only stop the outbreak, but leave behind strong systems that will be better at finding the disease and other threats, at stopping it before it spreads, at preventing it in the first place. In fact, if those systems had been there in the first place, we wouldn't be here today. The outbreak would have been over already.

We don't know how to treat Ebola, and we don't know how to vaccinate, we don't have medications that cure it, but we do know how to care for patients with Ebola. You may have seen a lot of press coverage about experimental treatment, and the plain fact is that we don't know whether that treatment is helpful, harmful, or doesn't have any impact, and we are unlikely to know from the experience of two or a handful of patients whether it works.

We do know that supportive care for patients with Ebola makes a big difference. Supportive care saves people's lives, giving them fluid, making sure they are not over or under their fluid balance, giving them supplemental oxygen if it is needed, treating other infections that occur, providing good quality healthcare.

We are currently coordinating with NIH, FDA, the Department of Defense, and others to see whether there can be new treatments and whether these treatments can be effective and available. But there is a lot we don't know about that yet. It is important that we keep in mind that we do know, even without medicines that are specific to Ebola or a vaccine, we do know how to control it, and we can stop it.

I want to spend a moment on what we are doing to protect people in this country. First off, the single most important thing we can do is to stop the outbreaks, to stop it at the source. The second issue that we are working on is to help these countries do a better job screening people who are leaving their countries so that they will screen out people who are ill or who may be incubating Ebola. And, third, because we recognize that we are interconnected, we are working closely with State and local health departments and health providers throughout the United States so that they are aware that there could be people who come from these three countries who have been there in the last 3 weeks, if they come in with fever or other symptoms, they should think that it could be Ebola, immediately isolate them in the hospital, and get them tested at CDC.

We have issued a Level 3 travel advisory against all nonessential travel to Guinea, Sierra Leone, and Liberia. We have issued a Level 2 travel advisory about enhanced precautions on Nigeria, and we will reassess the Nigerian situation daily or more frequently as needed.

There is strict infection control possible in hospitals in the U.S., and there has been some misconception about this. Ebola is not as highly infectious as something like influenza or the common cold. What is so concerning about Ebola is that the stakes are so high, that a single lapse in standard infection control could be fatal. That is why the key is to identify rapidly and strictly follow infection control guidance.

It is certainly possible that we could have ill people in the U.S. who develop Ebola while here after having been exposed elsewhere. It is possible that they could spread it to close family members or to healthcare workers if their infection is not rapidly identified. But we are confident that there will not be a large Ebola outbreak in the U.S. We are confident that we have the facilities here to isolate patients, not only at the highly advanced ones like the one at Emory, but really at virtually every major hospital in the U.S.

What is needed is not fancy equipment. What is needed is standard infection control rigorously applied. We have released guidance for doctors and other healthcare providers in the U.S. on identifying, diagnosing, and treating patients, and guidance for airline flight crews, cleaning personnel, and cargo personnel.

Fundamentally, to end here, we have three roads before us. We can do nothing and let the outbreak rage, and I don't think anyone wants to do that. We can focus on stopping these outbreaks, and that is something that we will certainly do. Or we can focus not only on stopping these outbreaks, but also on putting in place the laboratories, the disease detective, the emergency response systems that will find, stop, and prevent future outbreaks of Ebola and other threats.

We do face in this country a perfect storm of vulnerability with emerging infections like Ebola, resistant infections like the ones we discussed in our last hearing, intentionally created infections, which remain a real threat. But we have unique opportunities to confront them with stronger technology, more political commitment, and success stories on real progress from around the world.

Earlier this year the U.S. joined with the World Health Organization and more than two dozen other countries to launch a Global Health Security Agenda. That Global Health Security Agenda is exactly what we need to make progress not only in stopping Ebola, but in preventing the next outbreak.

And the second document that we provided for you provides a summary of what the mapping is between what we launched back in February before this outbreak was known or reported to have started and what is needed to stop the Ebola outbreak, and they are closely aligned.

The President's budget includes a request of $45 million to CDC to accelerate progress in the detection, prevention, and response.

A former Under Secretary of State for Africa said to me, citing his decades of work, that CDC is the 911 for the world. And though I was happy to hear that, I realized that really what we want to make sure is that every country, or at least every region, has its own public health 911. That will be good for them, it will be good for us in terms of safety, it will improve economic and social stability, and expanding that type of work, strengthening global health security, will allow us to not only stop this outbreak, but also prevent future outbreaks and stop them faster if they do occur.

Thank you so much for your interest in this topic.

Mr. SMITH. Dr. Frieden, thank you very much for that very comprehensive and incisive testimony.

[The prepared statement of Dr. Frieden follows:]

House Committee on Foreign Affairs, Subcommittee on Africa, Global Health, Global Human

Rights, and International Organizations

Combating the Ebola Threat

August 7, 2014

Statement of Tom Frieden, MD, MPH, Director, Centers for Disease Control and Prevention

Good afternoon Chairman Smith, Ranking Member Bass, and members of the Subcommittee. Thank you for the opportunity to testify before you today and for your ongoing support for the Centers for Disease Control and Prevention's (CDC) work in global health. I am Dr. Thomas Frieden, Director of CDC. Just a year ago, I testified before this very Subcommittee about the importance of CDC's work to strengthen global health security by improving detection, response, and prevention. Today, I am here to discuss the current epidemic of Ebola in West Africa, which illustrates in a tragic way the need to strengthen global health security.

We do not view Ebola as a significant danger to the United States because it is not transmitted easily, does not spread from people who are not ill, and because cultural norms that contribute to the spread of the disease in Africa – such as burial customs – are not a factor in the United States. We know how to stop Ebola with strict infection control practices which are already in widespread use in American hospitals, and by stopping it at the source in Africa.

Ebola is a severe, often fatal, viral hemorrhagic fever. The first ebolavirus was detected in 1976 in what is now the Democratic Republic of Congo. Since then, outbreaks have appeared sporadically. The current outbreak in Guinea, Liberia, and Sierra Leone is the first that has been seen in West Africa and the biggest and most complex Ebola outbreak ever documented.

Ebola has an abrupt onset of symptoms similar to many other illnesses, including fever, chills, weakness and body aches. Gastrointestinal symptoms such as vomiting and diarrhea are common, and in approximately 45 percent of cases there is hemorrhaging, or serious internal and external bleeding. There are two things that are very important to understand about how Ebola spreads. First, the evidence suggests that Ebola only spreads through human-to-human transmission from people who are symptomatic– not from people who have been exposed to, but are not ill with the disease. Second, everything we have seen for the past few decades indicates that Ebola is not spread by casual contact; Ebola is spread through direct contact with bodily fluids of a sick person, or exposure to objects such as needles that have been contaminated. While the illness has an average 8-10 day incubation period (though it may be as short as two days and as long as 21 days), we recommend monitoring for signs of symptoms for the full 21 days. Again, people are not contagious during that incubation period. To be clear, evidence does not suggest Ebola outbreaks are spread through the air. Catching Ebola is the result of exposure to bodily fluids, which we are seeing occur in West Africa, for example, in hospitals in weaker health care systems and some African burial ceremonies. Getting Ebola requires exposure to bodily fluids of someone who is ill from – or has died from – Ebola.

The first recorded cases in the current outbreak were reported in March of this year. Following an initial response that seemed to slow the outbreak for a time, new cases flared again due to weak systems of health care and public health and because of challenges health workers faced in dealing with communities where critical disease-control measures were in conflict with cultural norms. As of earlier this week, the outbreak surpassed 1,600 cumulative reported cases, including nearly 900 documented deaths. The effort to control the outbreak in some places is complicated by fear of the disease and distrust of outsiders. Security is tenuous and unstable, especially in remote isolated rural areas. Just recently, health care workers were confronted by an angry mob, leading them to retreat back to safety.

Further, many of the health systems in these countries are weak, and do not reach into rural areas. Health care workers may be limited, or may not reliably be present at facilities, and those facilities may have limited capacity. Local traditions such as public funerals and cultural mourning customs including preparing bodies of the deceased for burial, make efforts to contain the illness more difficult. Furthermore, the porous borders among the three countries and remoteness of many villages have greatly complicated control efforts.

Though the outbreak began in March of this year, there have been several recent developments that have focused world attention on the situation. First, on July 20th, an American man who had previous contact with an Ebola infected patient boarded a plane in Liberia and flew to Nigeria. During that flight, the man exhibited symptoms; he was later diagnosed with Ebola and died five days later. Unfortunately, health care workers did not use infection control measures in caring for him before his Ebola disease was diagnosed. Second, many healthcare workers, including doctors and nurses, have been infected with the Ebola virus, over half of whom have died. Finally, in recent weeks two Americans working in Liberia with a humanitarian aid group have fallen ill with Ebola. Several organizations have scaled back or withdrawn volunteers from the affected areas, due to both health and security risks. These events have focused attention on the ongoing risk of the outbreak spreading to other countries, the need for constant vigilance in infection control procedures when in contact with patients, and the heroism and sacrifice of health care workers, and volunteers from the United States and around the globe, in the face of this dreadful and merciless virus. That is why great care is being taken to help the two American humanitarian workers who came back home for treatment. As we have done with similar cases in the past, we are helping to ensure, both in their transport and in their care at Emory University Hospital, that meticulous infection control procedures are being followed. Bringing humanitarian workers back home to the United States is the right thing to do to help save lives. The role of the public health system is to make sure that in doing so, we keep the risk of infection to the absolute minimum, both during transport and while they are in care here, and that's exactly what we have done and will continue to do.

CDC and our partners must surge to deliver resources and expertise to help end this outbreak. Far too many lives have been lost already. We have a difficult road ahead which will take many months, but we must redouble our efforts to bring this terrible outbreak under control.

Fortunately, we know what we must do. In order to stop an Ebola outbreak, we must focus on three core activities: find active cases, respond appropriately, and prevent future cases. The use of real-time diagnostics is extremely important to identify new cases. We must support the strengthening of health systems and assist in training healthcare providers. Once active cases have been identified, we must support patient care in treatment centers, prevent further transmission through proper infection control practices, and protect healthcare workers. Epidemiologists must identify contacts of infected patients and follow up with them every day for 21 days, initiating testing and isolation if symptoms emerge. And, we must intensify our use of health communication tools to disseminate messages about effective prevention and risk reduction. These messages include recommendations to report suspected cases and to avoid close contact with sick people or the deceased, and to promote safe burial practices. In Africa, another message is to avoid bush meat and contact with bats, since "spillover events", or transmission from animals to people, in Africa has been documented through these sources.

Many challenges remain. While we do know how to stop Ebola through meticulous case finding, isolation, and contact tracing, there is currently no cure or vaccine for Ebola. We need to strengthen the global response, which requires close collaboration with the World Health Organization (WHO) and additional assistance from our international partners. At CDC, we activated our Emergency Operations Center to respond to this outbreak, and are surging our response. One of the surge objectives is an initial deployment of fifty disease control experts in thirty days to the region to support partner governments, WHO, and other partners working in the region. Other goals during this thirty-day time period include:

- Improved case finding, contact identification, and follow up in each country, as well as improved database management to support these activities
- Improved health messaging in these areas, particularly targeting uncooperative communities
- Improved coordination with our partners, including WHO, Médecins Sans Frontières (or Doctors Without Borders), and country Ministries of Health.

Last Thursday, CDC issued a warning to avoid nonessential travel to the West African nations of Guinea, Liberia, and Sierra Leone. This Level 3 travel warning is a reflection of the worsening Ebola outbreak in this region. In addition to warning travelers to avoid going to the region, CDC is also assisting with active screening and education efforts on the ground in West Africa to prevent sick travelers from getting on planes. The United States receives 362 million travelers a year from other countries, and these travelers are essential to our economy, our families, and our communities. A very small proportion of world travelers entering the United States are coming from the affected nations. If a person exposed to Ebola becomes sick en route to or within the United States, CDC has protocols in place to protect against further spread of disease. These include notification to CDC of ill passengers on a plane before arrival, investigation of ill travelers, and taking steps to isolate travelers who are ill or believed to have been exposed. It is not impossible that there will be some travelers who become sick in this country, and as we have seen in the past week, hospitals and airports are able to identify and quickly respond to potential cases, even if they prove to be low-risk for Ebola. But we are confident that a large Ebola outbreak in the United States will not occur.

CDC also provides guidance to airlines for managing ill passengers and crew and for disinfecting aircraft. Last week, CDC issued Health Alert Notices reminding United States healthcare workers of the importance of taking steps to prevent the spread of this virus, how to test and isolate suspected patients and how they can protect themselves from infection.

Working with our partners, we have been able to stop every prior Ebola outbreak, and we will stop this one. It will take meticulous work. It's like fighting a forest fire: leave behind one burning ember, one case undetected, and the epidemic could re-ignite. Ending this outbreak will take time, at least three to six months in a best case scenario, but this is very far from a best case scenario. Once this outbreak is controlled, we will leave behind stronger systems to prevent, detect, and stop Ebola and other outbreaks before they spread. These include lab networks that can rapidly diagnose Ebola and other threats, emergency operations centers that can swing into action at a moment's notice, and trained disease detectives who can find an emerging threat and stop it quickly. If these people, facilities, and labs had been in place in the three countries currently battling Ebola, the outbreaks would already be over. We must do more, and do it quickly, to strengthen global health security around the world, because we are all connected. Diseases can be unpredictable – like H1N1 coming from Mexico, MERS emerging from the Middle East, or Ebola in West Africa, where it had never been recognized before – which is why we have to be prepared globally for anything nature can create that could threaten our global health security.

Global health security is a shared responsibility that cannot be achieved by a single actor or sector of government. In partnership with other nations and international organizations, the United States is committed to accelerate progress toward a world safe and secure from infectious disease threats and to promote global health security as an international priority.

There is worldwide agreement on the importance of global health security, but as the recent Ebola outbreak demonstrates, there is much more to be done. All 194 World Health Organization Member

States have adopted the International Health Regulations (IHR). Progress has occurred over the past years, but 80 percent of countries did not claim to meet the IHR capacity required to prevent, detect, and rapidly respond to infectious disease threats by the June 2012 deadline set by WHO. No globally linked, inter-operable system exists to prevent epidemic threats, detect disease outbreaks in real-time, and respond effectively. Despite improved technologies and knowledge, concerning gaps remain in many countries in the workforce, tools, training, surveillance capabilities, and coordination that are crucial to protect against the spread of infectious disease, whether naturally occurring, deliberate, or accidental. The technology, capacity, and resources exist to make measurable progress across member countries, but focused leadership is required to make it happen.

Earlier this year, the United States Government joined with partner governments, WHO and other multilateral organizations, and non-governmental actors to launch the Global Health Security Agenda. Over the next five years, the United States has committed to working with at least thirty partner countries (with a combined population of at least four billion people) to improve their ability to prevent, detect, and effectively respond to infectious disease threats - whether naturally occurring or caused by accidental or intentional release of pathogens. As part of this Agenda, the President's FY 2015 Budget includes $45 million for CDC to accelerate progress in detection, prevention, and response. The economic cost of large public health emergencies can be tremendous – the 2003 Severe Acute Respiratory Syndrome epidemic, known as SARS, disrupted travel, trade, and the workplace and cost the Asia-Pacific region alone $40 billion. The Budget's $45 million proposal would improve detection, prevention, and response and potentially reduce some of the direct and indirect costs of infectious diseases.

Improving these capabilities for each nation improves health security for all nations. Stopping outbreaks where they occur is the most effective and least expensive way to protect people's health. While this tragic outbreak reminds us that there is still much to be done, we know that sustained commitment and the application of the best evidence and practices will lead us to a safer, healthier world.

Thank you again for the opportunity to appear before you today. I appreciate your attention to this terrible outbreak and I look forward to answering your questions.

_____

Mr. SMITH. I would like to now yield to Dr. Pablos-Méndez.

STATEMENT OF ARIEL PABLOS-MÉNDEZ, M.D., ASSISTANT ADMINISTRATOR, BUREAU FOR GLOBAL HEALTH, U.S. AGENCY FOR INTERNATIONAL DEVELOPMENT

Dr. PABLOS-MÉNDEZ. Thank you very much, Chairman Smith, Ranking Member Bass, Chairman Wolf. Thank you for this opportunity, very timely, to allow the U.S. Agency for International Development to present to you an update on where we are with the work on this tragic and alarming outbreak of Ebola in western Africa. You have been a longstanding supporter of this area, and Member Bass quite so for Africa, so we couldn't have better champions in this emergency.

The epidemic of Ebola in western Africa is historic because both the magnitude is unprecedented, as well as because it has never really occurred in this region or, as we heard from Tom, spreading to cities and the risk of spread beyond the region.

I am, like many of you, saddened to see the devastation of the loss of lives caused by this outbreak, but also the broader social-economic disruption that this is inflicting in the region, what is really a set of fledgling democracies in western Africa.

The good news, as we have heard, is we know how to deal with Ebola. Since 1976 there have been about 30 or so outbreaks in central Africa, and each of those, of course, have been contained. The systems don't have to be perfect. The basics have to be in place. Systems have to be familiar.

Uganda has a track record that is worth noting. In the year 2000 they had about 425 cases during that outbreak. The support that we provided allowed that outbreak to be contained. Subsequent outbreaks in 2008 only saw 149 cases, a two-thirds reduction, and in the last outbreak in the region, 2011–2012, the number was only 32. So systems can learn, can prepare, can deal with this outbreak. We have done it many times, and as Tom has said, we know exactly what to do.

USAID, with the support that you gave us all along, provides routine funding to both CDC, the World Health Organization in Geneva and in Africa to have preparedness planning and response, and indeed that has been part of the machinery that has been put in place here. We support about 22 laboratories in 18 countries in Africa and Asia where almost 500 new viruses have been detected just in the last 5 years. So there is a lot of activity going all the time.

This particular virus of Ebola is, again, familiar to us, and as far as we can tell from a biological, genetic point of view, it is really the same virus. It is not that it is a new mutant virus that has taken on new powers. It is the same virus we are familiar with, but it has entered a new region and has entered perhaps, as we speculate, because bats that have been tested positive in central Africa are now also tested positive in western Africa.

This ecological dimension of the work that we do has to be kept in mind, and because of the novelty of this, neither the new systems or the people in western Africa and other health systems were experienced in dealing with the outbreak, which has helped contribute to the dimensions of this.

USAID has also targeted in this year the response in western Africa. We started earlier this year supporting with a $2.1 million investment to WHO, to UNICEF, and has been reinforced now with $12.4 million to support CDC, the WHO, and the like.

Indeed, it is important to note, to Chairman Wolf's comments, that the outbreak in Sierra Leone and in Liberia probably started, in retrospect, we now with regard to verbal autopsies can see that earlier on, but the cases were identified in late March and for a couple of weeks we have had this outbreak that then went down. So that in the spring the initial outbreaks went down, as Tom Frieden has pointed out, but if you allow one case in these remote areas, one case can reignite the whole thing, and indeed that is what we have seen with a secondary spike that has been truly difficult to control.

These investments have allowed us to work with WHO and UNICEF to allow to deploy 30 or so technical experts, provide additional operational support, including 35,000 sets of personal protective equipment and supplies. Also the basics, soap, water, that sort of thing is also very important in this type of situation, and it is taking place as we speak.

USAID is closely coordinating its response to Ebola with the Departments of State, Health and Human Services, and Defense, as well as with WHO. The CDC has the lead in the response to the Ebola outbreak, but the coordination—and I have been part of many other interagency efforts—has been truly exemplary, and I want to really point that out. It has been something the last couple of weeks that that coordination has been working just to make sure that we actually support those countries to stop this outbreak.

USAID, in addition, has activated a Disaster Assistance Response Team, a DART, something that you are familiar with that we have deployed in other emergencies, from Fukushima typhoons to Haiti earthquakes, and this provides the architecture for the response of the U.S. Government once the U.S. Ambassador on the ground has declared an emergency. And this has indeed occurred, and the DART is now deployed, and the team, the team leaders and the deputy team leaders are in place. CDC is responsible for the health and medical part of this response, but there is plenty of other activities in planning, in operations, in communications, engaging not only in the USG, but with the other local governments and with the other partners that I mentioned before.

I spoke with our mission director in Liberia where we have a large platform for health work that works very closely with the Minister of Health. We have only one or so health staff in Sierra Leone regular in Guinea, and in Sierra Leone we did not have a mission. And so it has been we are building out of this DART and working with the CDC and others to have the required staff and experts on the ground to facilitate the report.

I want to report that the morale is high in our teams. Although the family members have been ordered to leave the country, our teams are staying put, working with the CDC, working with MSF, working with others, taking all the precautions to ensure their safety, but also supporting them to work effectively against this outbreak.

And this reminds us, of course, that an outbreak requires also prevention, not only in the acute setting to avoid the growth of this epidemic, but also the global vigilance that we must maintain since these viruses know no borders.

In the short term it is a humanitarian imperative and a national security priority to contain this Ebola outbreak as quickly as possible. It will take probably months to end it, but I think we can turn around these tables in the next couple of weeks if the proposed response that has been mounted is deployed and executed as planned. The U.S. Government is fully engaged in the response, and we are confident that we can stop the epidemic. As I said, it will not be easy and it might take several months.

In the long term we must assist developing countries in strengthening their own health systems, both those dedicated to infectious diseases like this, but also the overall capability of the systems to deal, because it is about the front line health workers in primary care settings, in communities, and this time is Ebola in western Africa. We have seen H1N1 coming from Mexico, we didn't expect that, or MERS coming from South Africa. These pathogens can jump anywhere, and health systems need to be prepared to deal with these things as they occur.

With your support, USAID will continue to make this a priority in our global health investments in Africa, and as Tom Frieden has alluded also, the administration is working on the Global Health Security Agenda for which we look to work with you in the plans because they will require support in the future, and we look forward to working with you on that. Thank you very much for giving me this opportunity, and I look forward to your questions.

Mr. SMITH. Doctor, thank you very much for your testimony and for your leadership.

[The prepared statement of Dr. Pablos-Méndez follows:]

Ariel Pablos-Mendez, MD, MPH
Assistant Administrator for Global Health
U.S. Agency for International Development

House Committee on Foreign Affairs
Subcommittee on Africa, Global Health, Global Human Rights, and International
Organizations
August 7, 2014

"Combating the Ebola Threat"

Chairman Smith, Ranking Member Bass, and Members of the Subcommittee, thank you for inviting me to testify on the response of the U.S. Agency for International Development (USAID) to the Ebola outbreak in Africa. Thank you also for your support for USAID's humanitarian and development programs, in particular our global health work.

Introduction

The ongoing Ebola outbreak in West Africa is the largest and most-protracted ever recorded and it shows no signs of waning as the affected countries have been unable to control the outbreak on their own. Since December 2013, Guinea, Liberia, Nigeria, and Sierra Leone have reported more than 1,600 confirmed probable and suspected cases. New cases continue to be recorded indicating that the outbreak – which has an overall fatality rate of 55%– has not been contained. I am truly saddened to see the devastation and loss of life caused by the outbreak, and I would like to express my condolences to those who have been affected or lost loved ones. This outbreak is severe, but it can be controlled, and the U.S. Government is working to confront this tragedy with a serious response to address the threat and assist affected countries in their response.

The spread of the deadly Ebola virus in Liberia, Guinea and Sierra Leone is also a reminder of the vast development needs that persist in some of the region's poorest countries despite rapid economic growth and investment. As a development agency, USAID is very concerned about the current Ebola outbreak in West Africa – and its potential for expansion – because of the health, economic, and social impacts this disease is having in the affected countries. We are guided by our Agency's mission statement - we partner to end extreme poverty and promote resilient democratic societies while advancing our security and prosperity – in our efforts to support countries' efforts to build their resilience to this threat. Countries that already have limited ability to provide health care for their citizens can ill-afford to lose health care workers to sickness and death, have health facilities close, or have other health and development priorities affected by the outbreak.

USAID's targeted response to the current Ebola outbreak in West Africa is appropriately an immediate response to the crisis at-hand. However, there also needs to be longer-term response that reflects the importance of monitoring and diagnosing viral threats that originate in animals. Such a response is critical to ensure future reoccurrences of the virus are contained prior to transfer to humans, where possible. In addition, it's critical that we build on ongoing health systems strengthening efforts, which help ensure a viral outbreak is contained at the earliest stages through improved access to care, health workforce training, and enhanced communication once diagnosis is made.

The lack of previous experience with Ebola virus in the affected countries has severely hampered efforts to contain the outbreak. Because Ebola had previously appeared in East and Central Africa, prevention and systems strengthening efforts that might have held the virus at bay and reduced its spread and terrible impact were not in place in West Africa. The initial delayed detection of the virus allowed it to spread and communities and health care workers have not had the information and necessary supplies to reduce their risk of being infected.

Targeted Response to the Current Ebola Outbreak

The current total USAID funding dedicated to the Ebola response in West Africa is $14.55 million since March 2014 when the outbreak was first reported. In partnership with the World Health Organization and UNICEF, we provided an initial $2.1 million to support the deployment of more than 30 technical experts, provide operational support for response efforts, including 35,000 sets of personal protective equipment and supplies (including hygiene kits, soap, bleach, gloves, and masks), and distribute information on Ebola virus to the general public and health workers. This equipment provides critical protection for those working on the frontlines of pandemic outbreaks – preventing human exposure to highly pathogenic viruses and other emerging infectious diseases by limiting the risk of animal-to-human and human-to-human infections during outbreak investigations and response, human case detection and treatment, as well as other activities. The funding to the World Health Organization builds on a $1 million annual investment that USAID has made since 2009 to enable responses to priority pandemic prevention and response.

On August 4, the U.S. Ambassador to Liberia declared a disaster due to the effects of the Ebola outbreak. In response, USAID has activated a Disaster Assistance Response Team (DART). The DART, comprising team members in Monrovia, Liberia, and Conakry, Guinea, will coordinate planning, operations, logistics, administrative issues, and other critical areas of the interagency response. The U.S. Centers for Disease Control and Prevention (CDC) will staff public health and medical response positions on the DART. An initial DART member is already on the ground in Monrovia, and the DART Team Leader arrived in Monrovia on August 6. Additional DART staff will arrive in-country in coming days. To further facilitate coordination, USAID and CDC will exchange liaison officers in the Emergency Operations Centers in the United States.

This week, USAID announced an additional $12.45 million of Global Health and International Disaster Assistance funding to support efforts by CDC, the World Health Organization, and NGOs to ramp up the Ebola response. Specifically, this funding will go toward the expansion of Ebola outbreak programs in the affected countries. These programs will provide technical experts to assist in outbreak response, help trace people who may be infected with the disease, as well as provide health clinics and households with hygiene kits, soap, bleach, gloves, masks, and other supplies to help prevent the spread of disease. USAID also has an additional 70,000 sets of personal protective equipment already in central and southern Africa that can be deployed to West Africa for use in the Ebola outbreak.

USAID is closely coordinating its response to the Ebola outbreak in West Africa with the U.S. Departments of State, Health and Human Services, and Defense along with the World Health Organization and other donors. Mechanisms have been established for U.S. Government coordination in the field and in Washington. As part of the larger package of support from the U.S. Government, USAID is currently assessing what additional assistance may be needed.

Foundational Investments in Combatting Pandemic and Emerging Threats

In this modern, interconnected world, threats old and new need to be continually monitored because they cannot necessarily be contained in their country of origin. More than a decade ago Severe Acute Respiratory Syndrome (SARS), which began in southern China and lasted about seven months, killed more than 900 people in 29 countries. Some estimates of the cost to the global economy were above $40 billion. Ebola and Marburg viruses in Africa, the H7N9 avian influenza in Asia, and the novel Middle East Respiratory Syndrome (MERS) coronavirus in the Middle East remind us that pathogens of animal origins can and do emerge and can quickly spread across the globe. While they typically recur, they can be controlled if the general public, health workers, veterinarians, and wildlife specialists are appropriately educated on the threat and containment and if health systems are appropriately strengthened.

For decades, USAID has been a leader in the control and prevention of infectious diseases. Today, USAID-funded programs are pivotal in the fight against HIV/AIDS, malaria, tuberculosis, neglected tropical diseases, pandemic influenza and other emerging threats – and the Agency is prepared to work with other partners in the U.S. government and elsewhere to transform the current threat in West Africa into another story of resilience in the face infectious disease, with Congress' support.

Recognizing that diseases such as Ebola, H5N1 and H7N9 avian influenzas, and MERS and SARS Coronaviruses periodically spill over from animals to cause outbreaks (and sometimes pandemics) in humans, USAID invested a total of $1 billion since 2005, including $72.5 million in FY14, in its Emerging and Pandemic Threats program that is strengthening the capacity of 18 countries in Africa and Asia to more-quickly and effectively detect and respond to viral threats, including Ebola. The program is testing samples from more than 21,000 animals and USAID has identified over 500 new viruses related to ones known to cause disease in animals and people. This program grew out of USAID's initial response to H5N1 avian influenza in 2005 and is working to identify interventions to reduce the risk of the animal viruses spilling over and spreading in human populations. The strategy of preventing human infectious with animal viruses by reducing viral spread in animals has been very successful for H5N1 avian influenza.

The Global Health Security agenda is an effort between the U.S. government, other nations, international organizations and public and private stakeholders, to accelerate progress toward a world safe and secure from infectious disease threats and to promote global health security as an international security priority. As part of this agenda, USAID is focusing on hotspots of previous disease emergence in countries and epidemiological zones where the risks of spillover, amplification and spread are greatest. As a result of USAID's efforts, capacities of local animal and human health staff and laboratories to detect, prevent and respond to diseases have been strengthened in 18 countries where new pandemic threats are most likely to emerge. We have developed regional networks in Africa and Asia involving more than 65 veterinary, medical, public health, and environment schools to train future practitioners in the fields of public health, medicine, veterinary sciences, and ecology in Africa and Asia to address future threats. The Agency is developing and testing a Public Health Emergency tool with the World Health Organization and CDC and is actively supporting countries in Africa to develop national preparedness plans to respond to threats such as Ebola. Critically, USAID is also working to address behaviors which contribute to disease threat for specific high-risk populations.

At present the program is focused on East and Central Africa as well as South and Southeast Asia, a strategic decision to invest in a targeted set of the highest risk countries to get maximum impact for our investments. If there are resources, the viral surveillance methodology and the Public Health Emergency tool could be applied to West Africa to expand detection and response capacities.

Foundational Investments in Health Systems Strengthening

With many villagers across Africa living great distances from health facilities or lacking transport to reach them, frontline health workers are often the first and only link to providing essential health services. In many cases during this outbreak, health workers were not equipped or trained to manage Ebola in West Africa underscoring the critical need for investment in health workers and health systems.

Guinea, Liberia and Sierra Leone are among 83 countries worldwide that the World Health Organization in 2013 reported to have below the minimum ratio of doctors, nurses and midwives (22.8 per 10,000 population) needed to provide basic health services to a population, and severe inequities in workforce distribution also exist within these countries. The World Health Organization and the Global Health Workforce Alliance estimate at least 7.2 million doctors, nurses and midwives are currently needed globally – a gap that could creep to nearly 13 million by 2035

In addition to the need for an adequate number of health care providers, all health workers need to be well trained in infection control protocols equipped with knowledge about transmission, and then provided with the needed equipment and supplies to fully implement their knowledge and skills. USAID has supported the development of occupational health and safety guidelines in numerous countries, and partners with international health organizations also dedicated to protecting the health of health workers, such as the International Council of Nurses and their Positive Practice Environments Campaign. The state of the health workforce and health systems of the affected countries hampers the ability of these countries to respond to the Ebola outbreak – but these countries are hardly alone in having inadequate training, support and numbers of health workers, especially in the rural areas where this outbreak took hold.

We are beginning to see a greater focus on health workforce and systems from many countries that are critical for both responding to disease epidemics and to providing the essential care that can save millions of lives every year. For example, 55 countries last year made concrete commitments to how they will improve their health workforce, including Guinea and Liberia.

U.S. investments are strengthening the global health workforce, increasing the capacity of African states to prepare, monitor and respond to disease outbreaks, but the Ebola outbreak highlighted serious gaps that remain.

Conclusion

Healthy, productive citizens are essential for global economic growth and regional security. Sound health systems are able to address pandemic threats. Our investments in health systems are made as part of efforts to address health needs in areas as diverse as HIV/AIDS, infectious diseases like malaria, tuberculosis, pandemic influenza and other emerging threats, child and maternal health and nutrition, and family planning and related reproductive health – but they pay dividends across sectors, including with respect to infectious diseases such as Ebola.

This outbreak in West Africa is a sobering reminder of the lethal consequences of limited infectious disease surveillance and response capacities in any country. The outbreak also reminds us that infectious diseases require prevention efforts and global vigilance, as they know no borders. It is a humanitarian imperative and national security necessity to contain the current Ebola outbreak as quickly as possible. The best investment the global community can make to prevent or mitigate future outbreaks is to assist developing countries to strengthen their own health systems, including infectious disease detection and response capacities. This is a core competency of USAID and, in coordination with other U.S. Government partners, we will continue to make this a priority within our Agency's development efforts.

Thank you very much for giving me the opportunity to testify. I look forward to your questions.

Mr. SMITH. I would like to note we have been joined by Augustine Ngafuan, who is the Foreign Minister of Liberia.

Thank you for being with us today, Mr. Minister.

And now I would like to yield to Ambassador Williams.

STATEMENT OF THE HONORABLE BISA WILLIAMS, DEPUTY ASSISTANT SECRETARY, BUREAU OF AFRICAN AFFAIRS, U.S. DEPARTMENT OF STATE

Ambassador WILLIAMS. Thank you very much, Chairman Smith, Ranking Member Bass, Chairman Wolf, and members of this subcommittee, for the chance to testify before you on this very important topic.

The evolving Ebola crisis in Guinea, Liberia, Sierra Leone, and now Nigeria is one of the most daunting challenges those countries and the region have faced in decades. To date, more than 1,600 suspected and confirmed cases of Ebola have been reported, including over 900 total deaths.

Although these affected countries are home to many heroic and dedicated health workers, the rapid spread of the disease reflects the lack of national capacity, particularly in the three epicenter countries of Liberia, Guinea, and Sierra Leone, to limit the spread of the disease and to treat patients. The NGO community, which has played a significant role in the response effort by providing front line medical care to patients, is hard-pressed to continue to provide care in all affected regions.

Compounding the issue, affected populations' lack of understanding of the virus and widespread mistrust of healthcare providers and treatment methods have further hampered response efforts. In significant portions of the affected regions, local traditions, such as public funerals and cultural mourning customs, including preparing bodies of the deceased for burial, have contributed to the spread of the virus and have led locals to block access to patients and in some places have led to attacks on healthcare workers. Following one such incident in Liberia, major care providers like Samaritan's Purse have begun pulling out of the region due to concerns for the safety of their staff.

Thus, in addition to proper medical care, there is an urgent need for effective health messaging campaigns and public outreach as an integral and crucial component of these response efforts. We are reaching out to ensure our response is coordinated with the WHO and other countries that can assist both through our representatives at WHO headquarters in Geneva and through direct discussion with other governments.

Guinea, Liberia, and Sierra Leone are still rebounding from lengthy conflict. These conflicts destroyed lives, institutions, and infrastructure. This was especially acute in Liberia and Sierra Leone, where the fighting went on for years. These countries have taken important steps to reverse the effects of deterioration and neglect and to build lasting security and stability. Border control and other factors key to checking Ebola's spread also are challenging for the countries in this region.

Aside from our interest in making sure this Ebola virus does not spread to the United States or farther in Africa, we do not want the virus to erode the capacity of African countries to address other important national and regional challenges. We want to ensure these countries remain strong, strategic allies to the United States in a region facing serious development and security challenges. Sadly, this virus already has impacted peacekeeping in Somalia. The African Union cancelled a planned deployment of Sierra Leonean peacekeeping force due to fears that the virus could be introduced into the country.

Given the critical importance of this issue, we are fully committed to doing everything possible to shore up each government's efforts to combat the viral outbreak and control its spread. We are confident that through the concerted and coordinated efforts of our Government and our international partners we can contain and stop this virus. In fact, Mr. Chairman, the Department has established a monitoring group on the humanitarian situation in west Africa to monitor and coordinate information. The task force may be reached at the following email address, that is taskforce-5@state.gov.

Since the beginning of the crisis the Department has maintained close contact and coordination with the governments of all of the affected countries and has closely monitored their operational plans to combat the viral outbreak. In Sierra Leone, President Koroma directed government officials to make containment of the virus their top priority and set up a Presidential task force to lead the government's efforts. In Guinea improved messaging to the populace helped healthcare providers gain access to infected regions. And in Liberia, President Johnson Sirleaf announced a national task force to combat the spread of the virus.

On August 1, the three Presidents detailed their collective strategy for eradicating the virus in a joint communique following a meeting of them of the Mano River Union. We commend all three countries for taking this outbreak seriously and for taking concrete steps to address it.

This week's news of new cases in Lagos, Nigeria, a city of over 20 million people, makes the need for an effective, well-supported, and well-coordinated national plan and international response more important than ever. In fact, Mr. Chairman, I just met today with President Blaise Compaore of Burkina Faso and with Dr. Kadre Ouedraogo, who is president of the ECOWAS Commission, who told me that the health ministers of the three affected states will meet again, they will meet in Conakry at the end of this week on August 11 through 14, and that following that the health ministers of all of the ECOWAS states will meet in Accra, Ghana, on August 28. The intensified attention of the health ministers of the entire region is a good sign, and it demonstrates that the whole region is seized with this crisis.

Assistant Secretary Linda Thomas-Greenfield has spoken to the Presidents of Guinea, Liberia, and Sierra Leone to express support and to assure them of our assistance to stop the spread of the virus. On August 4th, the Department hosted and moderated a meeting on Ebola on the sidelines of the U.S.-Africa Leader Summit to discuss the next steps for controlling and ending the virus. HHS Secretary Sylvia Burwell, CDC Director, my colleague here, Dr. Tom Frieden, and NIH Director, Dr. Francis Collins, USAID Assistant Administrator for Global Health Dr. Ariel Pablos-

Méndez, and President Alpha Conde of Guinea, the Liberian Minister for Foreign Affairs, Sierra Leone's Ambassador to the United States, and Professor Tomori Oyewale, the president of the Nigerian Academy of Science, participated in the meeting. Representatives from DOD, from the NSC, the World Bank, as well as private partners like the GE Foundation and Becton, Dickinson and Company, also joined. In addition to emphasizing the need to focus on detection, isolation, and adequate training for health workers in the field, we also emphasized our long-term commitment to building the health care capacities of individual west African nations beyond this immediate crisis intervention.

We continue to work with our international partners and the WHO to assess what is needed to properly treat patients and to mount a sustainable response. Such support has included providing financial and technical assistance to properly equip treatment centers and supporting communication efforts to help healthcare workers access affected communities. The WHO Sub-Regional Coordination Center opened in Conakry on July 23rd and is coordinating all surveillance efforts, harmonizing technical support, and mobilizing resources being provided to the affected countries. The organization has also launched a $100 million emergency response plan to surge resources to mount a more effective response. We are in continuous discussions to find new ways to provide assistance.

The Department of State has no higher priority than the protection of U.S. citizens. We extend our deep sympathies to the family of Patrick Sawyer, a U.S. citizen who died in Nigeria after contracting the virus in Liberia. At least two additional citizens affiliated with the response organizations have been infected in Liberia and are currently undergoing treatment. We are in close contact with the sponsoring organizations of those two individuals, and our thoughts and prayers go out to them and to their families.

U.S. Embassies in the affected countries have disseminated security messages, including the CDC's warnings, to resident and traveling U.S. citizens. We continue to take steps to educate citizens about the virus, to dispel rumors, and to provide information on preventive measures.

We also take the safety and well-being of our staff very seriously. To that end, the Department's Chief of Infectious Disease traveled to west Africa to provide Embassy staff with assistance regarding protection measures and case recognition. Additionally, Embassies in the affected region have organized regular town hall meetings to answer questions and concerns of mission personnel and U.S. citizens.

Embassies in neighboring countries like Mali, Senegal, and Togo have also held meetings to assess the capabilities of their host governments and to make contingency plans for Embassy personnel and resident citizens in the event of an outbreak.

In closing, Mr. Chairman, I would like to reiterate and assure this committee that the Department of State takes the Ebola threat very seriously and we are fully dedicated to working with our governmental and non-governmental allies, the interagency community and host governments in the affected countries to respond to this crisis, prevent its spread and to restore stability to the region.

I thank you for your attention to this issue, and I look forward to answering your questions.

[The prepared statement of Ambassador Williams follows:]

**Testimony by Deputy Assistant Secretary Bisa Williams,
Bureau of African Affairs, U.S. Department of State
House Committee on Foreign Affairs
Subcommittee on Africa, Global Health, Global Human Rights, and International
Organizations
August 7, 2014
*"Combating the Ebola Threat"***

Thank you very much Chairman Smith, Ranking Member Bass, and Members of the Committee, for the chance to testify before you on this important topic. The evolving Ebola crisis in Guinea, Liberia, Sierra Leone, and now Nigeria is one of the most daunting challenges those countries, and the region, have faced in decades. To date, more than 1,600 suspected and confirmed cases of Ebola have been reported, including over 900 total deaths.

Although these affected countries are home to many heroic and dedicated health workers, the rapid spread of the disease reflects the lack of national capacity, particularly in the three epicenter countries of Liberia, Guinea, and Sierra Leone, to limit the spread of the disease and to treat patients. The NGO community, which has played a significant role in the response effort by providing front line medical care to patients, is hard-pressed to continue to provide care in all affected regions. Compounding the issue, affected populations' lack of understanding of the virus and widespread mistrust of healthcare providers and treatment methods have further hampered response efforts. In significant portions of the affected regions, local traditions such as public funerals and cultural mourning customs including preparing bodies of the deceased for burial have contributed to the spread of the virus, and have led locals to block access to patients, and in some places have led to attacks on healthcare providers.

Following one such incident in Liberia, major care providers like Samaritan's Purse have begun pulling out of the region due to concerns for the safety of their staff. Thus, in addition to proper medical care, there is an urgent need for effective health messaging campaigns and public outreach as an integral and crucial component of these response efforts. We are reaching out to ensure our response is coordinated with the WHO and other countries that can assist, both through our representatives at WHO headquarters in Geneva and direct discussion with other governments.

Guinea, Liberia, and Sierra Leone are still rebounding from lengthy conflict. These conflicts destroyed lives, institutions, and infrastructure. This was especially acute in Liberia and Sierra Leone where the fighting went on for years. These countries have taken important steps to reverse the effects of deterioration and neglect, and build lasting security and stability. Border control and other factors key to checking Ebola's spread also are challenging for the countries in this region. Aside from our interest in making sure this Ebola virus does not spread to the United States or farther in Africa, we do not want the virus to erode the capacity of African countries to address other important national and regional challenges. We want to ensure these countries remain strong, strategic allies to the United States in a region facing serious development and security challenges. Sadly, this virus already has impacted peacekeeping in Somalia. The African Union cancelled a planned deployment of a Sierra Leonean peacekeeping force due to fears that the virus could be introduced into the country. Given the critical importance of this issue, we are fully committed to doing everything possible to shore up each government's efforts to combat the viral outbreak and control its spread. We are confident that through the concerted and coordinated efforts of our government, and our international partners, we can contain and stop this virus.

1. Diplomatic Outreach and Host Government Efforts

Since the beginning of this crisis, the Department has maintained close contact and coordination with the governments of all the affected countries, and has closely monitored their operational plans to combat the viral outbreak. In Sierra Leone, President Koroma directed government officials to make containment of the virus their top priority, and set up a presidential task force to lead the government's efforts. In Guinea, improved messaging to the populace helped healthcare providers gain access to infected regions. And in Liberia, President Johnson-Sirleaf announced a national task force to combat the spread of the virus. On August 1, the three presidents detailed their collective strategy for eradicating the virus in a joint communique following a meeting of the Mano River Union. We commend all three countries for taking this outbreak seriously, and for taking concrete steps to address it. This week's news of new cases in Lagos, Nigeria – a city of over 20 million people – makes the need for an effective, well-supported, and well-coordinated national and international response more important than ever before.

Assistant Secretary Linda Thomas-Greenfield has spoken to the presidents of Guinea, Liberia, and Sierra Leone to express support and assure them of our assistance to stop the spread of the virus. On August 4, the Department hosted and moderated a meeting on Ebola on the sidelines of the U.S.-Africa Leaders' Summit to discuss the next steps for controlling and ending the virus. HHS Secretary Sylvia Burwell, CDC Director, Dr. Thomas Frieden, NIH Director, Dr. Francis Collins, USAID Assistant Administrator for Global Health Dr. Ariel Pablos-Mendez, President Alpha Condé of Guinea, the Liberian Minister for Foreign Affairs, Sierra Leone's Ambassador to the United States, and Professor Tomori Oyewale, the President of the Nigerian Academy of Science participated in the meeting. Representatives from, DOD, the NSC, the World Bank, as well as private partners like the GE Foundation, and Becton, Dickinson, & Co. also joined. In addition to emphasizing the need to focus on detection, isolation, and adequate training for health workers in the field, we also emphasized our long term commitment to building the health care capacities of individual West African nations beyond this immediate crisis intervention.

We continue to work with our international partners and the WHO to assess what is needed to properly treat patients and mount a sustainable response. Such support has included providing financial and technical assistance to properly equip treatment centers and supporting communications efforts to help health workers access affected communities. The WHO Sub-Regional Coordination Center opened in Conakry on July 23, and is coordinating all surveillance efforts, harmonizing technical support, and mobilizing resources being provided to the affected countries. The organization has also launched a $100 million emergency response plan to surge resources to mount a more effective response. We are in continuous discussions to find new ways to provide assistance. My colleagues from the CDC and USAID can provide you with additional details about our assistance to and support of the WHO during this crisis.

2. *Protection of U.S. Citizens*

The Department of State has no higher priority than the protection of U.S. citizens. We extend our deep sympathies to the family of Patrick Sawyer, a U.S. citizen who died in Nigeria after contracting the virus in Liberia. At least two additional citizens affiliated with response organizations have been infected in Liberia and are currently undergoing treatment. We are in close contact with the sponsoring organizations of those two individuals, and our thoughts and prayers go out to them and their families.

U.S. embassies in the affected countries have disseminated security messages, including the CDC's warnings, to resident and traveling U.S. citizens. We continue to take steps to educate citizens about the virus, dispel rumors, and provide information on preventive methods.

3. *Safety of Chief of Mission Personnel*

We also take the safety and well-being of our staff very seriously. To that end, the Department's Chief of Infectious Disease traveled to West Africa to provide embassy staff with assistance regarding protection measures and case recognition. Additionally, embassies in the affected regions have organized regular town hall meetings to answer the questions and concerns of mission personnel and U.S. citizens.

Embassies in neighboring countries, like Mali, Senegal and Togo, have also held meetings to assess the capabilities of their host governments, and to make contingency plans for embassy personnel and resident citizens in the event of an outbreak.

In closing, I would like to reiterate and assure this committee that the Department of State takes the Ebola threat very seriously and we are fully dedicated to working with our governmental and non-governmental allies, the interagency community, and host governments in the affected countries to respond to this crisis, prevent its spread, and restore stability to the region.

Thank you for your attention to this issue. I look forward to answering your questions.

Mr. SMITH. Thank you so very much, Ambassador Williams.

I do have a few questions I would like to pose to our distinguished panel, beginning first with Dr. Frieden. As you said, supportive services are important. With no effective vaccine or drug treatment, you outlined how important those services are, including hydration and, I am sure, antibiotics to deal with some of the other co-infections.

Now, I wonder if you could just tell us, is there any disproportionality in result when it comes to whether or not we are talking about a frail elderly person, a woman, a man, a child, a woman who happens to be pregnant, or any of the others who has a compromised immune system? What has been the MO of that, if you could?

Secondly, I know that treatment centers, for example, in Guinea—there are some three to four treatment centers, but, again, it is very hard for people in that country as well as the others—Liberia and Sierra Leone as well—to get to those treatment centers. It is a long trek. Very often with the ride, the person is very sick, others could come in contact with him or her. There seems to be an overwhelming need.

One of the points that I think needs to be underscored that is under-appreciated in many places is that, in dealing with someone who is dying, especially in those—that part of the world, there is a psychological trauma with being alone. So it almost exacerbates the spread of the disease because people want to be around, near, touching and, when that person is highly infectious, that is when family members and others might get it. If you could, speak to that.

The lack of testing, testing areas, whether they be, you know, as part of the treatment centers where there is a testing lab—it is my understanding, especially since this masks and parallels what other—you know, it looks like other things, but it is Ebola—but unless you get that test back—how long does it take to do the test? And, again, is there any way of standing up labs?

I know for a fact that—you know, especially through the work of Bush's PEPFAR program, which has been followed up with Obama doing the same thing—and, you know, the idea that building health capacity and labs in Africa is a very high priority, and now we are seeing where inadequate labs or lack of labs leads to people being sick and not even knowing it.

The courage of the healthcare workers I think needs exclamation points. I know you are there as well and you go on the front line yourself and go into—all three of you—into contagious areas. But Dr. Brantly and Ms. Writebol and others who put their lives on the line, motivated so often by faith, in the case of Dr. Brantly and—I mean, I have read some of the things his wife has put out, the prayers that are being offered up not just for him, but for all of the victims.

In Liberia, there have been 60 healthcare workers infected. 35 are dead. In Guinea, 33 healthcare workers affected. 20 are dead.

How does a country now attract or retain healthcare workers who say, "If I go into that arena, the prospects of me getting this are very real"? Is there enough protective equipment, you know, the gowns, the plastic, to mitigate the possibility of transfer?

And, finally—and I do have other questions, but I will yield to my colleagues—there are a number of, I said in my opening, promising drugs. ZMapp is one of them. TKM—Ebola, which was in Phase I trials; yet, the FDA has a hold on it. They were contracted by the Department of Defense.

From what I have read—and it is only from what I have read, you know, the available data, it was showing promise. And I am wondering if there is any way to accelerate, knowing that you don't want to obviously put something out there that is risky—because Ebola is not 100 percent fatal, as we all know. We don't want to keep people getting sick from the remedy or supposed remedy.

What about accelerating that? Is there an effort to do that?

And my final question is about the safety of airline flight. Many people have contacted my office to ascertain, you know, how safe it is to fly perhaps next to somebody who has maybe changed flights en route to the United States coming from Liberia, for example.

And are the efforts at the airports, particularly where there is a large diaspora population—I don't know if you have enhanced efforts there where people from west Africa are more likely to go. But, you know, are they up to the task of detecting at point of embarkation of passengers who might be sick from Ebola?

Dr. FRIEDEN. So let me try to quickly give you clear answers to all of those questions.

The first is the relative case fatality rate of different groups. And in the current outbreak, the data is still too foggy for us to give you clear data. There is not the kind of robust data that we will have eventually, but don't have now to give you, what we would call a case fatality rate for different groups.

But there is one very intriguing historical fact which I think is worth mentioning. In 1967, there was a laboratory accident in Marburg, Germany. The Marburg virus was then identified. Marburg has a similar fatality rate to Ebola, if anything, a little higher. It is around 80 percent. The outbreaks have been in the 80 percent range in Africa.

The case fatality rate in Germany in the Marburg outbreak was 23 percent. Now, that might have been because of the better supportive care—there was no specific antiviral treatment—or it might have been because people were healthier going in. We don't know.

But we do know that it was dramatically different, and I think that is an important point. Good supportive healthcare is a proven way of saving lives, and we should never lose sight of that.

Second, in terms of treatment centers, you are absolutely correct that there is a challenge in getting to treatment centers. And that is one of—that is, in fact, the number one priority for the DART team, which USAID is convening and CDC is leading the medical public health aspects of, which is on the ground today in Liberia to assess.

And the biggest challenge is both in the city of Monrovia, where there continue to be chains of transmission, and in that tri-country area. So looking at whether one facility or multiple facilities and where the facilities would be, that is a critical issue for us to determine in the coming days.

Treatment centers, as you point out, are very important to support. I was speaking with the American Charge from Sierra Leone, who was speaking very movingly about the patients and their isolation in the treatment centers and simple things like giving them cell phones so they could talk to their family or things that they could do while there was very important. And if patients don't believe that they are going to be well-treated in the treatment centers, they won't come in and they may continue to spread it in the community. So good quality care is very important.

In terms of testing, you are absolutely correct. As you know, Mr. Chairman, with support from PEPFAR, the CDC has helped create the African Society for Laboratory Medicine, and that has for the first time ever had high-quality laboratories established all over Africa. These countries have not been PEPFAR-focused countries; so, they have limited activities in that area.

But scaling up laboratory testing is important. We will do that in two ways, first, by finding laboratories—this isn't simple laboratory tests. This is a realtime PCR. The results come back within a day, but false contamination, false positives, are possible if you are not scrupulously careful. And that would be a real problem.

So we will scale up the labs that can do testing. We are working with international partners on this, who are involved and with the Defense Department, which has a very active program, for example, in Sierra Leone and is providing services there, and with the National Institutes of Health, which has been very helpful.

We will also establish safe specimen transport means. We have done this in Uganda, where we can very safely transport. Hard to get a lab out all over, but quite possible to get transport into the lab. And that is what we will establish in the coming days.

In terms of the courage of healthcare workers, I certainly agree with you. And it is an issue not just for healthcare workers, it is an issue for patients. We have heard that, with healthcare systems less functional, problems like malaria may become more deadly.

So the impacts of Ebola aren't just Ebola. There are the other conditions that aren't treated because of Ebola. So responding is so very important, and protecting the responders is so very important.

So a key aspect that we are working on with the World Health Organization, with the countries, with USAID and others is making sure that there is effective personal protective equipment there for healthcare workers. We believe it is possible to take care of Ebola patients, even in Africa, safely, but it takes meticulous attention to detail.

In terms of the promising drugs, I can assure you that the U.S. Government is looking at this very carefully and will look at any way to try to expedite development or production, but I don't want any false hopes out there. Right now we don't know if they work and we can't, as far as we know, have them in any significant numbers. We hope that that might change.

But these medicines that have been used in the experimental cases, as far as I understand it, are not easy to use. They require infusion. They may have adverse events. And basic supportive care needs to be in place as a prerequisite to giving many of these treatments.

So whatever else we do, we have to do the basics right. And we might or might not have effective and available treatment in 3 months or 6 months or 1 year or 5 years, but we today have the means to stop the outbreaks.

And, finally, in terms of airline flights, we do have teams in the affected countries who are working with the equivalent of their border protection services, helping them to do screening at the airports. It is not a simple measure. It is key first to reduce the number of cases. That is what is going to be the safest.

And there are other things that can be done at airports in terms of questions to be asked or temperatures to be taken or lists to be cross-matched against known patients and known contacts, but all of those procedures do take time to set up. But we do have teams working on them now.

Mr. SMITH. Dr. Frieden, if I could ask you, if somebody is in proximity to a sneeze or a cough, is that a mode of transmission?

Dr. FRIEDEN. In medicine, we often say, ''Never say never.'' So, in general, the way we have seen the disease spread is by close contact with very ill people.

As you know, the individual who traveled from Liberia to Lagos did become ill on the plane, and we have assisted those countries to track the travelers who traveled with him and, as of now, have not identified illness in any of them.

But, in general, it is not from a sneeze or a cough. In general, it is from close contact with someone who is very ill, but we do have concerns that there could be transmission from someone who is very ill.

Mr. SMITH. So at the fever stage, if somebody is onboard, that wouldn't be construed to be very ill? You are not likely to get it from somebody who is at fever stage?

Dr. FRIEDEN. You are not going to get it from someone who is not sick with Ebola. So if they are just clearing their throat or sneezing or coughing, but they don't have a fever, they have not become ill with Ebola, they are not infectious to others. But if someone became ill on the plane and was having fever or started bleeding, then, for example, that might present a risk to those who came in contact with that and didn't take appropriate precautions.

Mr. SMITH. Is there a way of advising airline personnel, particularly flight attendants who, again, might be in very close proximity to the whole plane and there could be someone on there? Does CDC advise them and the airlines, like Delta, which flies numerous flights to the region?

Dr. FRIEDEN. Yes. We have provided detailed advice to the airlines.

Mr. SMITH. Let me just ask you, Ambassador Williams, very quickly.

You spoke—and I think it was a very good insight—about the handling for funeral arrangements and just generally sensitivity to the culture.

I know it is part of the public information campaign in Guinea—for example, some 9 million cell phones are being used and text messages are being sent with a number for the Red Cross, and one of the text messages says, ''The bodies of Ebola victims are very contagious. Do not manipulate. Call the Red Cross.''

Now, I am wondering if there is any thought being given—I remember after Operation Provide Comfort, when the Kurds made their way fleeing Iraq after Saddam Hussein—I was there about 5 or 6 days after that, and our military was on the ground and they were using PSYOPS to educate and leafleting that was done in a way that we would use in a not-so-benign situation. In this case, it was to get food out and Meals Ready to Eat, and it was amazing how that kind of information made the Kurds who were at great risk of the elements and starvation, very aware of what they needed to do.

Is there any thought of helping the Liberians and the other countries with a benign PSYOPS effort to make people aware? I know that radio is being used, but it seems to me that more needs to be done. Any thoughts?

Ambassador WILLIAMS. Thank you, Chairman.

I can't say that we have moved to the point of PSYOPS, but I think you are hitting a very, very important issue, which is that culture makes a difference and you have to adjust your messaging and do the campaign according to the sensitivities and the routines and the practices per culture.

What was extremely effective in Guinea was not only what you mentioned, Mr. Chairman, but the fact that they started talking about survivors and the survivors came on the radio. They went around and said: ''Look, I was sick, but this and this and this happened to me. I did such and such, and I am still alive. You should go get treatment. You should isolate. You should make sure people know you have this.'' So that is very, very important.

Our military right now is helping in the ways that have already been described as far as with logistics and making sure that we can get in body bags, protective equipment for the healthcare providers. And that—that is where we are so far.

But we are relying upon the host governments to help explain to us what is most effective, what the sensitivities are, and what messaging needs to get out. And then we were helping with the means of the communication, but not the actual message, because they know best what the people need.

Mr. SMITH. Thank you.

I yield to Ms. Bass.

Ms. BASS. Thank you very much, Mr. Chairman.

This is for the doctors. I wanted to know if you could talk a little bit more about the disease. We all know about fevers, but having spent a number of years working in emergency rooms, I can imagine what is happening in our emergency rooms around the country. Everybody with a fever is running in, being concerned.

And I was wondering if you could talk a little bit more about what are the other symptoms of the disease and maybe if you have any thoughts of why some folks are surviving, since my understanding of part of the disease is that it interferes and takes over with the immune system.

Dr. FRIEDEN. So the fevers can be one symptom, but chills, weakness, nausea, vomiting, diarrhea are other symptoms. In about 45 percent of cases, there is bleeding, both internal and external, and that is a feared complication. So these are symptoms which, as you both pointed out, are not specific to Ebola.

And that is why the laboratory testing is so important. It is also why it is not the case that someone will know they have Ebola and go to a special Ebola unit and why it is so important that health facilities who are there think of the risk of Ebola and then rapidly isolate people.

In this country, what we have told healthcare workers to do is take a travel history: Has the person been in one of these countries in the past 21 days? If yes and if they have fever or other symptoms, then do tests.

We have already had five people in different parts of the U.S. who come in with a travel history to one of these countries in the past 21 days. All five have turned out not to have Ebola. Two had malaria, one had influenza, and two had something else.

So we expect this to happen. In fact, we want there to be a high-level index of suspicion so that doctors will rapidly isolate the person and then rapidly test them.

Ms. BASS. And how do you screen? Just as the chairman asked—and I know, you know, again, what is in the press is that, if someone on an airline sees someone with a fever—and I mentioned to you yesterday when we spoke there are these pictures in the news of the wands or they are doing some type of screen, and I think you pointed out—and maybe you could talk about that is really not effective.

So how does one screen, short of a blood test in a medical facility, that like an airport worker might do?

Dr. FRIEDEN. There is no way to diagnose Ebola without a laboratory test. So if someone has fever and they may have been exposed, they have been in one of these countries, they need be isolated and tested.

For people within the U.S., currently both we have a test that is accurate and relatively quick—a few hours once the specimen gets to our lab—and the Department of Defense also has a test.

And we are working in collaboration with them to see if we can over the next couple of weeks get that test out to what is called the Laboratory Response Network, or LRN. This is a network that CDC coordinates of laboratories at mostly health departments around the country to test for dangerous pathogens.

Ebola is not in their usual network; so, this would be a new procedure. But either through the Defense Department's assay or our own, we will look into getting that available so not all of the tests have to come to CDC Atlanta and they can be tested locally. We also have safe ways for specimens to be transported to CDC if they need to be transported.

Ms. BASS. One of the other things that we have touched on a couple of times today is the ZMapp. I think that is what it is called. And I would like for you to talk a little bit about that because there is a lot of concern that maybe we have access to this and are not providing that access. And one of the things that I think was a mention that maybe you could elaborate is that there might only be just a couple of doses that—that were even made.

Dr. FRIEDEN. So, first, I really would need to refer you to the National Institutes of Health, which would be the lead on developing new treatments and vaccines against Ebola. The information I have on that medication is quite indirect.

What I understand is that it is a combination of different monoclonal antibodies—this is part of what the body does to respond to an infection—and that there is some evidence from at least one animal study that it may have some effect on the illness.

However, I think I would caution that we really don't know. I think that has to be emphasized. Even whatever happens with these two individuals—and we hope that they and every other person with Ebola will get better, as some people do. But we will not know from their experience whether these drugs work.

Antibodies are only one part of our response to an illness. There are many different parts of the immune response. In some other conditions, antibodies can actually make the disease course worse. So we don't know until it is rigorously studied scientifically.

I also cannot tell you definitively how many such courses there are. I have heard that there are a handful, fewer than the fingers of one hand, but I have no direct information on that. Other manufacturers are coming forward to say that they have some or could make some. We have heard from some companies that it would take months to make even a few dozen courses.

So I think this is rapidly changing information. I don't have definitive information and would refer you to the National Institutes of Health.

But let's always go back to the basics, that we know now how to stop Ebola and, if a person has Ebola, we know how to support them to reduce their risk of death in proven ways by treating and preventing other infections that they can get when they are sick by providing hydration, fluids, careful management of their health condition, blood transfusions if they need them. These are proven things.

If there is a new treatment, we will do everything we can to help get it out to those who need it most. We would also be very interested in a vaccine. If there were an effective vaccine, we would offer it with full informed consent to healthcare workers as a way of helping them protect themselves.

But right now we are months or at least a year away, from everything I have seen and heard, from significant quantities of either drugs or a vaccine, even if everything goes well and we are able to develop them. That could change, but that is the information as of now. What is available to us today right now is the means to stop the outbreaks in Africa.

Ms. BASS. It is not helped when it is reported that the one individual had a miraculous turnaround and was able to walk out of the ambulance because he had gotten the treatment. You know, that leads to the belief that there is some kind of cure out there that we know about that we are not sharing.

In looking at the death rates at the different countries, there is a difference. In Guinea, it is 74 percent; Sierra Leone, 42; and Liberia, 55.

And I wanted to know from the panelists, what do you see as causing the difference? And is it a situation where each of the countries have addressed the outbreak differently? Capacity? Commitment? What is the difference?

Dr. FRIEDEN. I think, in terms of the death rates, the data is still very fluid and it is not clear that each of those rates is actually comparable, given the different ways cases are diagnosed and counted and reported.

What is the case is that, for each of the countries, they have their own challenges. I would say that the country of Guinea is probably furthest along in responding. They have reduced their number of cases. But there, too, they have continued spread in healthcare facilities.

And that tri-border area, that area seems to be a core epicenter. And security problems in Liberia, for example, have led to treatment facilities not being available in Liberia, patients moving over to Guinea and then re-importing the disease there.

So it really is a regional response that is needed for the three countries, and that also will be a core first deliverable of the DART team that USAID is leading and CDC is leading the public health healthcare medical aspects of to identify in that region what can be provided rapidly to assist with caring for patients to allow us to reverse the outbreak.

Dr. PABLOS-MÉNDEZ. Just, if I may add, in addition to the difficulty in establishing the denominator to calculate the percentages that Tom is referring to, the fact is that across, nonetheless, even if there were more cases that we have not recognized, that is more likely to be recognize the cases. And so the percentage can vary in that.

But, on the whole, we are seeing that the disease is indeed quite deadly, but not universally fatal. And that is very important.

And, in Guinea, it has been a very important part of the study of educating the public because, if people think that you are going to get it, you are going to die, then there is no motivation to go to the services, to protect the families. And so the education has been paramount.

And, in Guinea, we have seen a plateau of the outbreak. In the last month or two, there is still some, especially because of the border area. But, on the whole, the response that Guinea has implemented and the education in this case has been very important both for the patients, again, and for the health workers.

We are now doubling up to 70,000 the personal protective equipment will be available. We had already in storage in Ouagadougou in the region, and that is what we got going through the spring. We are having more now equipment that is to be prepared to protect those health workers.

And it was raised before and I want to emphasize, health workers are trying to do their best to save lives of other people. And so the 120-plus of them who have already died in this outbreak are true heroes. And I think that support for the health workers is really paramount, and I think that we are very committed to doing that.

When we mentioned earlier the State Department has advised the families of our staff to leave the countries, it is not so much because they are in immediate risk, but because the health system's already so overwhelmed that, if you had anything else, there is nowhere for you to go to.

And, in addition, for many of those, if I may add, also, is that kids who will start school soon, the schools may not be opening. So asking the family members to leave is wise, not because they are in immediate danger.

Ms. BASS. You know, Dr. Pablos-Méndez, I think you have mentioned a couple of different figures, and maybe I have confused them.

I think you said 70,000 and 35,000 pieces of protective gear. And I was wondering if those have reached the affected—well, number one, what was the difference? Did I get them mixed up? Or maybe it was at different times.

And then, two, has it reached the area? Because I mentioned yesterday earlier speaking to President Johnson and she was very concerned and expressed the need for additional units of protective gear.

Dr. PABLOS-MÉNDEZ. Thank you.

The 35,000 units were indeed part of the first batch that we mobilized early on in the epidemic. We already had some of them in strategic storage locations, one in the region, in Ouagadougou, that has been made available now.

The question is the logistics of distribution, and that is where our DART team now deployed will support the countries to make sure that they reach all the front line workers that would require it. But with the additional resources we are mobilizing now, we will reach 70,000 of such; these are spacesuits that you have seen.

Ms. BASS. Right.

Dr. PABLOS-MÉNDEZ. It is the production part, and they have to be prepared. They don't come just ready to use. And that is where we are right now. But we expect to reach 70,000 of such PPEs, as we call them, to reach where important.

We have also in every countries some of this training. We have some of those available to them just at least to become familiar in case that we need to scale up.

And we have all along model how this could spread. Indeed, as Nigeria has been one of the nodes, Ghana has been another that we are paying attention because, in our models, that suggest that that could be a route where the airlines flights could allow this to escape the countries that we have even today. So we are preparing and we have trainings and we have some of the equipment already available there.

Ms. BASS. Thank you.

Ambassador Williams.

Ambassador WILLIAMS. Yes. Thank you.

I just wanted to clarify. As I said earlier, we are continuously monitoring the situation in all of the affected countries. And our primary responsibility, our primary concern is the health and welfare of American citizens abroad, our Embassy staff as well as residents.

We have not, in fact, ordered the departure of our family members from any of our places, although we are—it is—of course, it is one of the things that occurs to people. It is one of the things under consideration. But at this time we haven't.

And I know that, since we do have an interagency coordinating committee that has been talking about a number of things, it has been among the things we have been considering, but——

Ms. BASS. So USAID has had the——

Ambassador WILLIAMS. No American personnel. No American official personnel or their families have been ordered. It is one of the—it is one of the options under consideration, but we are continuing to look.

As was stated, you know, our families, our dependents, follow the government officers all over. We are on the front lines every day all over in very dangerous places.

And bearing in mind the stresses in the various countries now and the concerns, the anxiety levels, among some of our families, it is something that has been discussed.

But at this point we have not ordered the departure of any of our family members. I just wanted to make sure you understand.

Ms. BASS. Okay. And the last question is—I think it might have been—one of the panelists referred to the security issues in Liberia, and, you know, when I spoke to President Johnson yesterday, she didn't mention that.

But when I was watching the news this morning, there were—you know, the text messages that come across the news said that she was very concerned about it.

And I wanted to know if maybe you could address—what are the security—what is happening? Is this something new? What are we talking about?

Ambassador WILLIAMS. What I was trying to stress is putting it in a framework. You know, these things happen in a context. And it is one thing to have this health crisis, but, in fact, the country was already still trying to build itself up from a rather torturous past.

Ms. BASS. Okay.

Ambassador WILLIAMS. So the President of Liberia did declare a disaster in her country as a result of this crisis because she really wants the international community to pay attention and she is trying to also explain to her people why she is mobilizing an intensified force to specifically focus on Ebola, but there is no new security external threats.

Ms. BASS. Okay. Thank you.

Thank you, Mr. Chairman.

Mr. SMITH. Chairman Wolf.

Mr. WOLF. I thank you, Mr. Chairman.

In what country did this first begin?

Dr. FRIEDEN. The first cases were reported from Guinea, but it is really possibly—we don't really know at this point—or I don't know at this point the history of it. But the epicenter is that forested area that has the confluence of the three countries.

Mr. WOLF. Ambassador Williams, over the years, we have heard from Ambassadors and Embassy staff that Washington does not take cables from them seriously.

When did the State Department in the District of Columbia in Washington first get a cable notification from the Embassies of Sierra Leone, Guinea and Liberia about the Ebola crisis?

Ambassador WILLIAMS. Chairman Wolf, if you don't mind, I am going to look through my notebook to see if I have the exact date. I am not sure I have the exact date. So if you could just give me a second.

Mr. WOLF. Sure.

Ambassador WILLIAMS. Mr. Chairman, I am going to have to look up the cable. I don't have the cable traffic.

I will say, however, we are in daily communication with our Embassies and, if not through cables, through emails, through telephone. We are in constant control. But I will find the specific answer to your question and get it back to you.

Mr. WOLF. You were an Ambassador. It is often we hear—and, as you know, my district in northern Virginia, we have many.

They say that sometimes the cable gets sent and they wonder if they are taken seriously. I would like to know when the cables were sent. And, secondly, how high in the State Department were the concerns raised, at what level and what time?

Ambassador WILLIAMS. Thank you.

And I will take the question. I have to find the exact date. We have been aware of this for a while now and we are working on it.

And as having come out of the region as an Ambassador—as it was stated, I was our Ambassador to Niger up until the end of 2010.

In covering west Africa in the Bureau of African Affairs, I am seized with this. I am paying close attention to what the Embassies are saying. I know what Ambassadors and the people there are going through. And I will get the answer to your question as soon as possible.

Mr. WOLF. You mentioned the work in response of USAID and State and others.

What other donor nations have gotten involved in the efforts? And what exactly are they doing? Can you give us a list of the countries?

You said, Dr. Frieden, you have 40 to 50 people coming.

Can you tell us what Great Britain is doing and what France is doing. Can you give us some specification as to numbers and how they are cooperating. It all cannot be the United States. What are our European allies and others doing, in numbers, if you can?

Dr. FRIEDEN. I think it would probably be best if we got back to you with details. It is something of a moving target.

I can tell you that the French, through the Institut Pasteur, have been very active. They have laboratory services and other services there.

The British have also been very active and have provided both resources and people on the ground. We had an announcement earlier this week from the World Bank of a commitment of $60 million to $70 million for emergencies as well as the emergency response as well as a longer-term response.

The World Health Organization, as you may be aware, issued an appeal recently for $100 million to respond to the outbreaks. And we have been in close coordination with many of our colleagues around the world.

Mr. WOLF. Has the White House asked them to be involved? For instance, the Germans have a history in Africa. The French have a history in Africa. The British have a history in Africa. Has there been a formal request by the White House to the heads of those governments that they participate to help your effort?

Dr. FRIEDEN. We have had intensive conversations with multiple other countries.

Were you going to say something, Dr. Pablos-Méndez?

Dr. PABLOS-MÉNDEZ. The answer is yes. The Ambassadors in Geneva had met from the various countries.

And, as you pointed out, there are many historical linkages, the British Government particularly supporting the response in Sierra Leone, France supporting the response in Guinea.

We have a strong presence, really, hand-in-glove, with the Ministry of Health in Liberia. So our response has been particularly important there, as Tom has mentioned.

The emergency plan that WHO put forward just over a week ago is for $103 million. They originally got about $30 million of that covered to begin moving, including some of the support that we have been providing.

With the World Bank coming through, also, just this week with an announcement of $200 million, that will allow us to fill the gap in the WHO plan for the immediate response, but, in addition, will invest in the months to come in strengthening the systems in that part of the world.

So many of these pieces and, as we speak, many of these things are moving very fast. So we are trying to continue that conversation. But in Geneva it has been a focus for the various donor countries to be having periodic updates as to how much more resources.

But that geographical location of division of labor, if I can put it that way, is already underway, even though CDC's presence is in all of these countries.

Mr. WOLF. Is the African Union engaged?

Dr. PABLOS-MÉNDEZ. The African Union has been engaged. The African Regional Office of the World Health Organization, in particular, has been engaged.

And to your earlier question, in Liberia, March 27 was when the first cases were reported. There was only a dozen or so of cases and then the outbreak fizzled. And this is typical of these outbreaks in central Africa. And for a month, there were not many new cases.

So, in fact, the early behavior of the outbreaks was light to begin, as we have seen in previous outbreaks, and it was only as it was rekindled again in this three-border area that we have seen the expansion, particularly in Sierra Leone and Liberia, whereas, in Guinea, it has been after the initial outbreak more a sense of containment.

Mr. WOLF. Are the Chinese involved? The Chinese Government has historically invested in soccer stadiums in Africa? Are they involved?

Dr. FRIEDEN. We would have to get back to you about their involvement.

Mr. WOLF. Madam Ambassador, can you tell us? You are with the State Department.

Ambassador WILLIAMS. Yes. I will have to look into that. I haven't heard about the Chinese involvement at this point, but I will check.

But I would like to reiterate—you were asking about the African Union—as I mentioned earlier, the ECOWAS states, the subset of the regional governments, are very seized with this and they are meeting this week and then again in 10 days after that.

Mr. WOLF. The last question, Mr. Chairman.

If someone wanted to raise a question or call somebody, do something, had a great idea, who do they call? Is there one person? Is it the CDC? Is it the Secretary of State? Is it USAID?

For our friends here in the United States, but abroad, is there one person and one place and one number that someone can call? Because on the 28th, it was very difficult, bouncing from here to there.

And let me just say again to Dr. Frieden. Thank you for taking the call, even as you were traveling.

Is there one place that we would go to or someone would go to?

Dr. FRIEDEN. For response to any potential case or problem here, that is the CDC. That is the——

Mr. WOLF. And what about if a nation abroad wanted to contribute, wanted to be involved, had an idea? Who do they contact?

Dr. FRIEDEN. In terms of the global collaboration, the key there is to support the World Health Organization, which really is the lead for the overall response.

Mr. WOLF. And is there an individual there at the World Health Organization who is responsible, that is your person to contact?

Dr. FRIEDEN. Yeah. That would be Dr. Keiji Fakuda.

Mr. WOLF. Okay. Good.

Thank you, Mr. Chairman.

Mr. SMITH. Before we go to the our next panel, if Ms. Bass has any additional questions, I will recognize her for that.

How accurate is the data? Data in even the best and most pristine of situations often is very hard to obtain. But here we are talking about proximity issues, difficulty of ascertaining what is really going on.

There was a report on CBS News that suggested that there may be as much as a 50 percent higher prevalence of Ebola. And I am wondering if you might want to comment on that. Is there any underreporting? And that is both of cases as well as fatalities.

And then, secondly, I know that the FDA is notoriously slow and notoriously comprehensive. And I don't want to either exaggerate or understate. But, ZMapp, TKM-Ebola and that one, again, was contracted by our own Department of Defense to work on that, and, yet, those clinical trials have been halted, Phase I.

And I am just wondering if there is any effort to rethink that. Because this could take off—you know, those who have lost their lives and are sick is a tragedy beyond words, but many more could become sick and die as a result.

Is there an interagency effort to say, ''Let's relook at that''? There might be some reason to lift that Phase I trial's halt to see if we ought to get at it.

And, finally, in his testimony today, Mr. Isaacs of Samaritan's Purse, again, the man with whom I and Congressman Wolf spoke to last week who had a profound sense of urgency and thought that we needed all to be doing more—he said it took two Americans getting the disease in order for the international community and the United States to take serious notice of the largest outbreak of the disease in history. Yesterday the President of Liberia declared a state of emergency in the nation. This declaration, he goes on, is at least a month late.

And I am wondering, not only with the countries that are already now affected, the four of them, what might be the fifth or the sixth? Is there a sense that there is a heightened concern about another nation, particularly one that might be contiguous with these four?

Dr. FRIEDEN. So in answer to your first question, yes, we think that the data are not as accurate as we would like. There may be cases counted as Ebola that are not, and there may well be many cases not counted that are.

The lack of treatment facilities, lack of laboratory facilities, make it so that the data coming out—it is kind of a fog of war situation, if you will. And that is one thing that we want to try to resolve quickly by getting laboratory, epidemiologic. But if there aren't treatment facilities, the patients won't come forward and we won't be able to do the control activities.

In terms of the FDA, there are calls at least once, sometimes four or five times a day on coordination. I can tell you that they are leaning very far forward on this and they are quite willing and quite constructive and productive in thinking of how to get things out there sooner if there is anything available.

I think, on the one hand, we have to do everything we can to try to find new tools. On the other hand, we have to recognize that we have the tools today to save lives and stop the outbreak.

And in terms of future countries, we can't predict where that might be, but we do know that an outbreak anywhere is a threat everywhere.

And one of the reasons we have focused on the global health security program is that we have the international health regulations, which require countries to report outbreaks and new diseases so that we can all, as a global community, work together because it is in all of our best interests not only to protect health, but to protect the economy, to strengthen our work in this area.

Mr. SMITH. I want to thank our very distinguished panelists for your extraordinary service for the sick and at risk and for being here today and helping to enlighten our subcommittee and, by extension, many other Americans who are tuning in and watching this. Thank you so very, very much.

Dr. FRIEDEN. Thank you.

Ambassador WILLIAMS. Thank you.

Mr. SMITH. I would like to now introduce our second panelists, beginning first with Mr. Ken Isaacs, who serves as the vice president of programs and government relations for Samaritan's Purse.

Ken Isaacs has served as the director of the Office of Foreign Disaster Assistance within USAID. He coordinated the U.S. Government's response to the Indonesian tsunami, the Pakistani earthquake, humanitarian relief efforts in both Darfur and South Sudan, as well as the Niger and Ethiopian emergency responses.

Mr. Isaacs has more than 27 years experience working in the relief and disaster response fields and has led major efforts in dozens of countries, including the ones I just mentioned. He is currently leading the Samaritan's Purse organization's efforts in Liberia in response to the Ebola epidemic.

We will then hear from Dr. Frank Glover, who is the director of the Urology Institute and Continence Center in the Urology Institute Ambulatory Surgery Center.

His discovery of the world's highest rate of prostate cancer in Jamaica has been internationally recognized and published in numerous journals and textbooks. He and his wife founded SHIELD, or Strategic Healthcare Initiative Emphasizing Local Development, which is dedicated to building a medical school in Liberia, training resident doctors in various medical and surgical specialties, and providing loan forgiveness for Liberian doctors that have trained in the United States and who would like to go back and be involved in teaching doctors and serving patients in Liberia. Dr. Glover has been involved in efforts to treat Ebola in Africa since the early 1990s.

Mr. Isaacs, please proceed.

STATEMENT OF MR. KEN ISAACS, VICE PRESIDENT OF PROGRAM AND GOVERNMENT RELATIONS, SAMARITAN'S PURSE

Mr. ISAACS. Thank you.

Chairman Smith, esteemed members of the council and fellow guests of this subcommittee, I am privileged to testify before you today on the developments of the Ebola outbreak in west Africa and Samaritan's Purse experience in response there.

I am going to read this first page so I don't overlook any of the things that I really want to say, and then I am going to put the script away and I am going to say the things that I feel like need to be said.

Samaritan's Purse is an international NGO with 38 years of experience, dedicated to humanitarian relief. We have worked in over 100 countries, including Afghanistan, North Korea, South Sudan, Sudan, Syria, and Liberia.

As an organization, we have responded to medical emergencies, such as the cholera epidemic in Haiti, and we have provided medical care to the people of Bosnia, Rwanda, and Sudan during the genocides in those countries.

The Ebola outbreak has had a profound impact on our organization, and I would like to share with you about our experience in Liberia. I want to take this opportunity to thank the United States Government, particularly the Department of State and the Department of Defense, for assisting Samaritan's Purse in the evacuation of our sick personnel from Liberia. We could not have done it without them.

And we would especially like to call to attention and thank Kathleen Austin-Ferguson of the Department of State, Dr. William Walters of the Department of State, Phil Skotte of the State Department, Mr. Dent Thompson, and Congressman Wolf and yourself.

We would also like to thank certain staff members of the CDC and the National Institutes of Health for bringing to our attention and obtaining the experimental medication as a treatment option for our two infected staff members.

As an organization, we have worked to contain the growing Ebola crisis in Liberia and we were devastated to discover that two of our personnel had contracted the deadly virus while trying to assist others.

The support that the U.S. Government has shown to our organization is tremendous, and Samaritan's Purse thanks you for helping us bring the two of them home in the face of incredible challenges.

The Ebola crisis was not a surprise to us at Samaritan's Purse. We saw it coming back in April. Our epidemiologists predicted it. By the middle of June, I was having private conversations with senior government leaders and, by July, I was writing editorials in the New York Times saying that this was out of control.

In the 32 years since the disease was discovered, as I believe Dr. Frieden said a moment ago, there were a total of 2,232 known infections, which killed 1,503 people. Easily, this present outbreak is going to surpass that in fatalities as well as overall cases.

It is clear to say that the disease is uncontained and it is out of control in west Africa. The international response to the disease has been a failure, and it is important to understand that.

A broader coordinated intervention of the international community is the only thing that will slow the size and the speed of the disease. Currently, WHO is reporting 1,711 Ebola diagnoses and 932 deaths in west Africa. Our epidemiologists and medical personnel believe that these numbers represent 25 to 50 percent of what is happening.

The Ministries of Health in Guinea, Liberia, and Sierra Leone simply do not have the capacity to handle the crisis in their countries. If a mechanism is not found to create an acceptable paradigm for the international community to become directly involved, then the world will be effectively relegating the containment of this disease that threatens Africa and other countries to three of the poorest nations in the world.

I know that a part of community and development philosophy is to work with your local partner and build capacity. The capacity that is needed in the nations that are fighting Ebola should have been built 3 to 5 years ago. But in the times of crisis, I believe that the attention needs to be put on the crisis and the building of the capacity should be a secondary function.

We undertook a massive public awareness campaign in Liberia starting in April and we have had over 435,000 people go through that training, but there are 3.6 million people there and the majority of them are illiterate. It is not going to be easy to change the way that people think and what their cultural mores are.

In the first months, we were able to provide support to the World Health Organization, the CDC, the Ministry of Health and Doctors Without Borders, also known as MSF, with our two aircraft, the only two aircraft in Monrovia, in Liberia, that were flying support.

We flew personnel, supplies, and specimens back and forth across the country. It makes a difference from the triangulation area that Dr. Frieden was talking about, also known as Foya, to Monrovia. It reduces it from a 16-hour road trip to a 40-minute helicopter flight.

I do want to take this moment to recognize and thank our co-workers in Doctors Without Borders for standing in the trenches with us. They are still in Sierra Leone. They are in Guinea. And they are now filling the gap for us in Liberia, as we have had to pull back while we re-plan what we are going to do next.

If there was any one thing that needed to demonstrate a lack of attention of the international community on this crisis, which has now become an epidemic, it was the fact that the international community was comfortable in allowing two relief agencies to provide all of the clinical care for the Ebola victims in three countries, two relief agencies, Samaritan's Purse and Doctors Without Borders.

It was not until July 26, when Ken Brantly and Nancy Writebol were confirmed positive that the world sat up and paid attention. Today we are seeing headlines every day of Ebola fears. There is a man who has bled to death, evidently, in Saudi Arabia. And the Saudi Government has confirmed it was a hemorrhagic fever, and he came from Sierra Leone.

There was a man, a Liberian-American, who came to ELWA Hospital with one of the most prominent physicians in Liberia, and that physician openly mocked the existence of Ebola. He tried to go into our isolation ward with no gloves, no protective gear. It is not an issue of gloves and a mask. It is an issue of no millimeter of your skin can be exposed or you will get sick and most likely die. That is sort of the reality of it.

Those two men left our hospital. They went to the JFK Hospital in downtown Monrovia, where the doctor did examine Ebola patients, and he was dead 4 days later. The other man was dead 5 days later, but not before he went to Nigeria. And now there are cases of death from Ebola in Nigeria and there are eight more people in isolation.

Our epidemiologists believe that what we are going to see is a spike in the disease in Nigeria and then it will go quiet for about 3 weeks and then, when it comes out, it will come out with a fury. As I am talking to you today, we are making preparations for a hospital that we support 263 miles north of Lagos on what they are going to do when Ebola comes to them.

To fight Ebola, I have identified four levels of society that need intensive instruction because they simply do not understand what is going on. One is the general public. The custom that they have of venerating the dead by washing the body—I am going to be graphic because I think people need to know—a part of that is kissing the corpse.

In the hours after death of Ebola, that is when the body is the most infectious because the body is loaded with the virus. Everybody that touches the corpse is another infection.

We have encountered violence against us on numerous occasions by people in the general public when we have gone out at the request of the Ministry of Health to sanitize a body for a proper burial. This is going to be a tough thing to do. So you have got this general awareness in the general public.

The number two area that needs to be addressed is community health workers. The entire international community has built a medical system around community health workers, which is essentially a moderately educated person who is given a few simple medical supplies, an algorithm chart, "If it hurts here—," "Are you passing blood?," "Do you have a temperature?," "Give them this color pills," "The doctor can talk about this more than I, but I think generally I am getting this right.'' They do not have the information to understand what Ebola is.

Friday—3 weeks ago this Friday at ELWA we had 12 patients with Ebola present. Eight of them were community health workers. Every one of those health workers had seen a patient, had diagnosed them for whatever they thought they had, and then they saw other patients. We have no way of knowing how many other people they have come in contact with.

The third level of society is actually medical professionals. Something needs to be done with a focused attention on medical professionals because, when I hear reports that prominent physicians who are educated and credentialed and respected denied the disease, I think they need a little bit more education.

And then the fourth level is leadership and politics, academics and religion. I don't know how to make those things happen, but those are the four stratas that I see to turn the disease back.

I think the entire fight on the disease has to be focused on containment. To contain it means you need to identify it. The previous panel up here was saying that it could be contained, that we have the information. Okay.

Liberia, Sierra Leone, and Guinea are poor. Like all countries, they have their problems with pointless bureaucracy, disfunction, and corruption. I know for a fact that, in Foya, the second largest center where Ebola is manifesting in Liberia, the workers at the Ministry of Health clinic were not paid for 5 months, even after the European Union had put money forward. The money just didn't get downstream.

Again, I will say that Ebola is out of control in west Africa, and we are starting to see panic now around the world. People want to know. I don't know about you folks. I look at the Drudge Report. It can drive a lot of panic.

And, you know, there is a guy in New York, there is a woman in England, there is—six people have been tested in the United States. There are reports that there are 340 Peace Corps workers coming back.

I greatly appreciate the help of the CDC. They have, in fact—Dr. Frieden and I personally have spoken, and they have, in fact, helped articulate their procedures and protocols for Americans returning into this country, and we are grateful for that.

While our Liberian office remains open doing public awareness campaigns, we have, in fact, suspended all other program activity. I would say that we are in the process right now of backing up, replanning, and reloading. We intend to come back and we intend to fight the disease more, but we have found some things that are needed.

One of the things that I recognized during the evacuation of our staff is that there is only one airplane in the world with one chamber to carry a Level 4 pathogenic disease victim. That plane is in the United States. There is no other aircraft in the world that I could find. That means that the United States does not have the capacity to evacuate its citizens back in any significant mass unless the Defense Department has something, the DoD has something that I am not aware of.

It was not easy to get the plane back, but one thing that is important is that if the United States, and I believe the United States is going to have to take the lead on this. It may not be popular for us to take the lead today, but I think that we need to take the lead. If we are going to expect people, including the CDC people, to go abroad and put their life on the line, there has to be some assurance that we are able to care for them if they are sick. That may be a regional healthcare facility that is exclusive to those citizens, and those workers, or that may be a demonstrated capacity to get them home. But one airplane with one chamber to get them back is a bit of a slow process.

Lastly, I think I want to say, it is a necessary thing that more laboratories be set up just in Liberia. The one laboratory now is at JFK Hospital. There is another one up over in Guinea in Gueckedou, and it can take us sometimes 30 hours to get a sample back. I have had discussion with the CDC about this. I think that is under consideration, but I would ask you if you could lean into that and question that, that would be very helpful.

The problem is, if you have six people that come in and three of them or four of them are suspected, you have to put them in a semi-quarantine area and you are holding that area of your case management center until you get a positive or a negative back on them and it takes time.

I understand that the World Bank has just committed $200 million to fight the disease. That is fine. That is good. It is a little late. It is good. As somebody with 26 years of experience, including being the director of OFDA running many DARTs around the world, interacting with governments on multiple levels, I have some practical questions. I would like to know where the money will go. I would like to know what it will actually produce and I would like to know what it will actually buy. I fear that money alone cannot solve this problem.

I disagree with earlier testimony that there is PPE in Liberia. That is inaccurate. I have an email that I have just received in the last 90 minutes from our hospital, the hospital that—the SIM hospital at ELWA. They are asking us for more personal protection gear. This is a problem everywhere. I am in touch daily with the headquarters of MSF, and Brussels. We are working hand-in-glove. I appreciate them so much for the way that they are stepping in and fighting this. The biggest challenge that we all have is the logistical support to get the materials and the supplies on the ground to fight this disease. As one of you quoted something that I said earlier, if we do not fight and contain this disease in west Africa, we will be fighting this disease and containing it in multiple other countries around the world, and the truth is, the cat is most likely already out of the bag.

I want to thank my staff, and recognize them for who have been there, and have done a valiant job at great risk to their own lives and I want to let you know that the reintegration back into their country is awkward, people are afraid to get around them. Their husbands and their wives don't know if it is safe to hug them. Their communities may ostracize them. We are doing everything that we can in the staff care way to give them a safe place to be, to protect their privacy, but I just want you to know how difficult it is for American citizens, and in fact citizens of all countries we have people on that team that came from more than six countries maybe seven countries. They all suffer these issues.

I believe that this is a very nasty bloody disease. I could give you descriptions of people dying that you cannot even believe. But I think that we have to fight this disease and we have to fight it now. We are going to fight it here or we are going to fight it somewhere else. I am talking about here in west Africa, but I do believe that an international coordinated response something significantly more is needed.

Thank you.

Mr. SMITH. Thank you very much, Mr. Isaacs, for that testimony.

[The prepared statement of Mr. Isaacs follows:]

Ken Isaacs

Vice President of International Programs and Government Relations, Samaritan's Purse

House Committee on Foreign Affairs: Subcommittee on Africa, Global Health, Global Human Rights, and International Organizations

Combating the Ebola Threat

August 7, 2014

Chairman Smith, esteemed members of this council and fellow guests of this committee; I am privileged to testify before you today on the developments of the Ebola outbreak in West Africa and Samaritan's Purse response.

Samaritan's Purse is an international NGO with 38 years of experience dedicated to humanitarian relief. We have worked in over one hundred countries including Afghanistan, North Korea, South Sudan, Sudan, Syria, and Liberia. As an organization, we have responded to medical emergencies such as the cholera epidemic in Haiti and we have provided medical care to the people of Bosnia, Rwanda, and Sudan during the genocides in those countries. The Ebola outbreak has had a profound impact on our organization, and I would like to share with you about our experience in Liberia.

I want to take this opportunity to thank the United States government, the Department of State, and the Department of Defense for assisting Samaritan's Purse in the evacuation of our sick personnel from Liberia. We would specifically like to call to attention and thank Kathleen Austin-Ferguson of the Department of State, Dr. William Walters of the Department of State, and Phil Skotte of the State Department, Mr. Dent Thompson, and Congressman Wolf. We would also like to thank certain staff members of the CDC and the NIH for bringing to our attention and obtaining the experimental medication used as a treatment option for our, two infected staff members.

As an organization, we have worked to contain the growing Ebola crisis in Liberia and were devastated to discover that two of our personnel had contracted the deadly virus while trying to assist others. The support that the United States government has shown to our organization is tremendous, and Samaritan's Purse thanks you for helping us bring the two of them home in the face of incredible challenges.

The Ebola crisis we are now facing is not a surprise to us at Samaritan's Purse, but it took two Americans getting the disease in order for the international community and the United States to take serious notice of the largest outbreak of the disease in history. Yesterday the President of Liberia declared a State of Emergency in the nation. This declaration is at least a month late.

Ebola is an incredibly infectious virus that begins with flu-like symptoms and can quickly develop into internal hemorrhaging. First discovered in 1976, the disease has predominately manifested in Uganda, Congo and South Sudan. In the 32 years since it was discovered (1976-2008) there were 2,232 known infections which killed 1503.[1] Until this current outbreak, the virus has never appeared in heavily populated areas but is now attacking the major cities of Sierra Leone, Liberia, Guinea and Nigeria. Lagos, Nigeria, alone has a population of 25 million people and the other cities have populations exceeding two million each. The infection and death rates of this recent West African outbreak will easily and quickly surpass the combined total of all previous outbreaks. The disease is uncontained and out of control in West Africa.

---

[1] Bulletin of the World Health Organization, Ebola Haemorrhagic Fever in Zaire, 1976: Report of an International Commission, 56 (2): 271-293 (1978). World Health Organization, Ebola Virus Disease, West Africa Update http://www.who.int/csr/don/2014_07_31_ebola/en/, July 31, 2014.

A broader coordinated intervention of the international community is the only thing that will slow the size and speed of the spread of the disease. Currently, WHO reports 1,711 Ebola diagnoses and 932 deaths in West Africa. We believe the reported numbers only show 25-50% of the cases.

The Ministries of Health in Guinea, Liberia and Sierra Leone do not have the capacity to handle these crises in their countries. If a mechanism is not found to create an acceptable paradigm for the international community to become directly involved, then the world will be relegating the containment of this disease that threatens Africa and other countries to three of the poorest nations in the world.

Samaritan's Purse initially focused its efforts on a massive public awareness campaign in which over 430,000 have been reached, but there are over 3.6 million people in Liberia and the literacy rate is very low. We had hoped to not become involved in direct clinical care but as the disease resurged in June, we had no choice. We began operating case management centers in the two most directly affected areas of the country: Foya and Monrovia.

In the first months, we provided support to WHO, CDC, MOH, and MSF with our two aircraft as we flew personnel, supplies and specimens back and forth across the country. We consulted closely with these organizations in establishing our Case Management Centers (Ebola isolation wards) and greatly appreciate their help. I want to take this opportunity to recognize the bravery and dedication of MSF for being in the "trenches" with us.

In mid-June, I began speaking privately to US officials that the disease was spiraling out of control and more needed to be done immediately. In mid-July, I published an op-ed article in the NY Times calling for an increased and accelerated response to this horrific disease.

Samaritan's Purse and MSF continued to be the two primary care givers, MSF in Guinea and Sierra Leone and SP in Liberia. That the world would allow two relief agencies to shoulder this burden along with the overwhelmed Ministries of Health in these countries testifies to the lack of serious attention the epidemic was given.

It was not until Dr. Kent Brantly and Mrs. Nancy Writebol were identified as Ebola positive on July 26th that serious international attention was paid to the crisis. Both individuals served on the Samaritan's Purse Ebola response team and both became gravely ill. With the help of the Department of State and other American government agencies we were able to arrange their air evacuations to Emory University Hospital for continued treatment where they still remain.

Treatment of Ebola requires personnel with knowledge and tools, but those medical professionals require assurance that if they become sick, they have the option to be adequately treated. During the evacuation of the two members of our team, it came to my attention that there was only one plane in the world with the ability to safely transport a patient with a level four pathogenic disease. The United States needs the capacity to evacuate multiple citizens at a time.

Over the last two weeks, it has become clear to the world that Ebola is out of control as we read headlines daily of new or potential cases in multiple countries including the United States. Responding to the disease exceeded the total capacity of SP in Liberia even though we had direct assistance from WHO, MSF, MOH, CDC and 400 of our national staff. We have removed all expatriate personnel and returned them to their home countries. While our Liberian office remains open, all program activity has been suspended except for ongoing Ebola awareness campaigns. We are no longer able to provide clinical patient care, and MSF has stepped into that gap. We are in the process of planning our return into Liberia to continue the fight.

The global impact of Ebola has yet to be fully realized. In the developing world, it has the potential to destabilize entire countries while creating widespread and even regional insecurity. It will have a devastating effect on transportation hubs, economies, healthcare systems, and governments.

The affected areas of West Africa are gripped with superstition, denial, fear and hysteria. Containment of the disease cannot happen without changing the attitudes and knowledge of four levels of society: the general public, healthcare workers, medical professionals, and leadership.

Liberia is full of cultural practices that propagate the spread of the disease, the biggest being the veneration of the dead, including the washing and kissing of the corpse. The corpse of an Ebola victim is at its maximum point of contamination in the hours immediately following death. Every contact with it will result in another infection. This practice is so strongly held that our staff has been faced with violence when the ritual was threatened by attempted collection of a corpse for sanitized burial.

The health care delivery system is built upon the CHW (community health worker), who is most often a moderately educated individual with basic knowledge to identify most commonly present diseases. The symptoms of Ebola are fever, joint pain, diarrhea, and vomiting. Unfortunately these are probably also the symptoms for over half of all diseases they normally encounter. This puts the CHW in the untenable position of having direct exposure to multiple Ebola patients without the knowledge to recognize the disease and the equipment to protect them. Two weeks ago, we had 12 Ebola cases present to our isolation center in one day, and 8 of the 12 were community health workers. We had no way of knowing how many people they may have contacted before they came to us for help. A special campaign is urgently needed to focus on this select group of health care providers.

The medical profession, that is trained physicians and nurses, also frequently lacks knowledge of Ebola and denies that it is real. We have had nationally known Liberian physicians come to our case management center in Monrovia attempting to examine Ebola cases without wearing any personal protective equipment. We were told by the staff of one prominent doctor that he openly mocked the existence of the virus to his coworkers. A close associate of his was the Liberian/American who traveled to Lagos, Nigeria. These two gentlemen went to the isolation ward at JFK Hospital in Monrovia where the doctor reportedly examined Ebola patients. Both men were dead within a week, one man taking the disease to Nigeria. These men were highly educated, credentialed and respected professionals, yet they did not believe in the existence or the seriousness of the disease. University students in Monrovia today continue to mock and deny the existence of Ebola. These behaviors will not allow the disease to be contained.

These behaviors reflect the need for cultural and societal changes that can only happen with the full support of political, academic and religious leaders. Liberia and West Africa need to have an immediate, concerted and significant effort to educate leaders of government, education and religion to recognize what Ebola is, how it is spread, preventative measures, and what to do if they or a loved one are exposed to the disease so they can prominently and publicly educate others. Certainly Sierra Leone, Guinea, and all of the countries that touch them are in need of the same education and awareness.

The fight against Ebola has to focus on the concept of containment. The virus, regardless of where it came from, now resides on planet Earth and it has the capability to travel at the speed of an airplane. Until there is a vaccine or a cure, we can only fight it by containing it, treating its victims, practicing proper hygiene, and educating.

The Ministries of Health of Liberia, Sierra Leone and Guinea are well intentioned but ill equipped. They face all of the challenges of other countries, such as pointless bureaucracy, corruption, and general dysfunction. While it should be the goal of the developed world to build capacity, the building of this capacity should not be the focus during times of an emergency crisis of a deadly disease that threatens the international community. There needs to be an immediate global coordination which allows the temporary transfer of authority of the national Ministries of Health to an entity to oversee the regional health crisis in order to save lives and stop the international spread of the disease. The entity to lead that coordination must be nimble, effective, resourced, and solely focused on managing the fight against the disease. I know of no such entity that exists today.

The international community should recognize that the Ministries of Health have a primary responsibility for the health of their citizens and a valuable role to play in managing the crisis but at times of great severity, the MOH cannot be expected to carry the lead role.

The World Bank has just committed $200 million to fight the disease. From my 26 years' experience working in global crises and disaster, I wonder where the money will go, what it will actually produce, and what it will actually buy. I fear money alone cannot solve this problem.

Lastly, it is vital that the necessary research and development of a successful vaccine and treatment for Ebola and other hemorrhagic diseases be aggressively sought through research and trials.

In the meantime, it is a nasty, bloody disease that we must fight now.

Thank you.

65

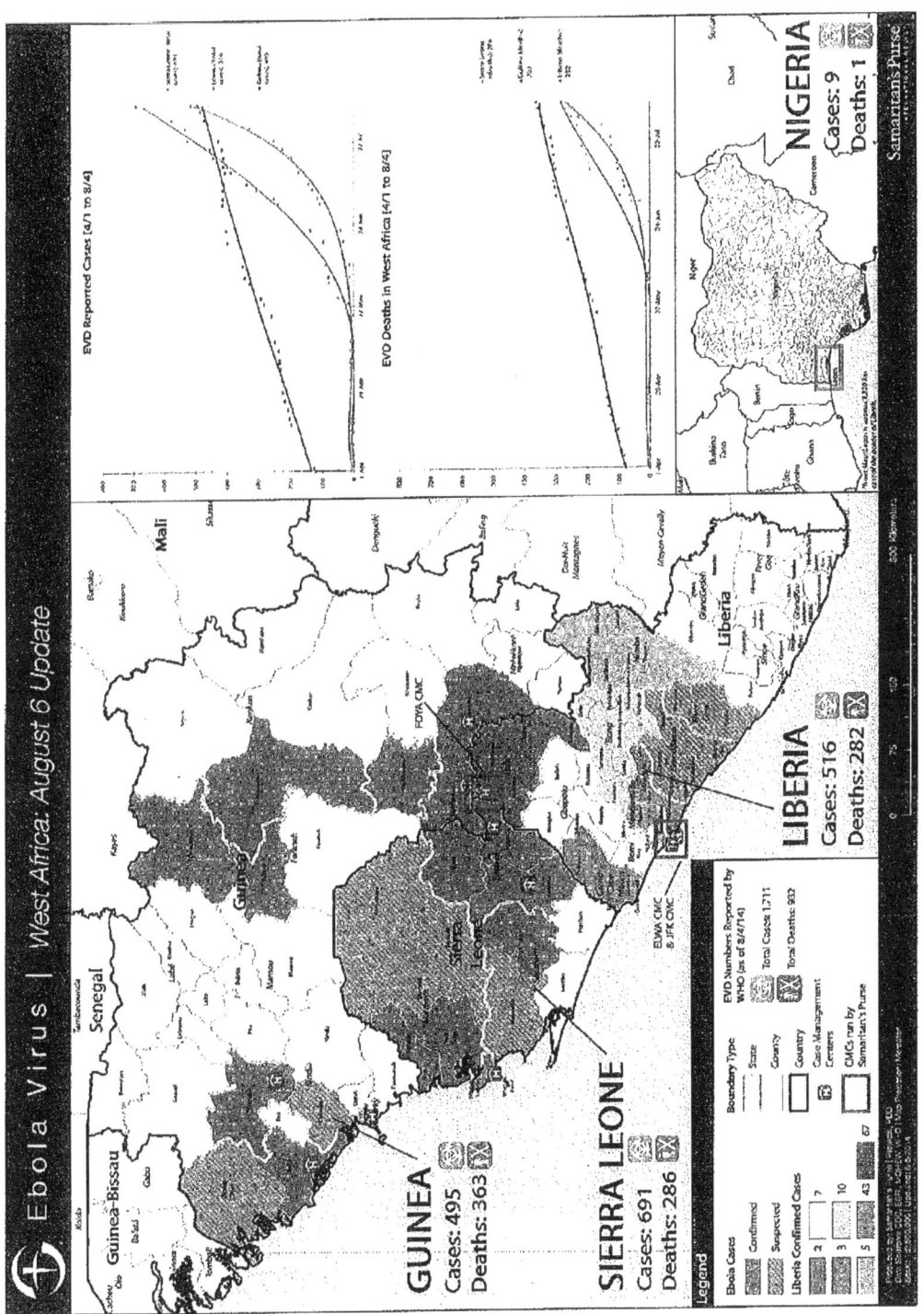

Mr. SMITH. And again, I think, underscoring your experience as head of the Office of Foreign Disaster Assistance, I mean, you have lived it and I don't think your resume tells the full story, all of those years of dedication.

So, again, thank you, and we will take extraordinarily serious your recommendations and the questions you have posed. And I thank you for it.

Dr. Glover.

STATEMENT OF FRANK GLOVER, M.D., MISSIONARY, SIM

Dr. GLOVER. Thank you, Mr. Chairman, and Members of Congress, for the opportunity to share with you.

My name is Dr. Frank Glover and I am a board certified urologist. I earned my M.D. degree at Johns Hopkins and also a Doctor of Public Health in International Health (Health Systems). I have also done some work as a research fellow at Johns Hopkins in epidemiology. I am also a medical missionary working with SIM, which is a Christian missions organization with works in over 60 countries.

In addition to working with SIM, I am the President of SHIELD In Africa, a U.S.-based NGO working in Liberia. My first experience in Liberia was in 1988, when as a medical student, I spent 2 months doing medical missionary work in an SIM hospital called ELWA (Eternal Love Winning Africa). For the past 3 years, I have spent 4 months per year working in various hospitals throughout Liberia. I have taken teams of up to 50 doctors and nurses several times per year. During this time period, we have taken care of thousands of medical and surgical patients. I have spent time rendering services of teaching, training, and patient care in most of the counties in Liberia. I have, therefore, had the opportunity to assess many of the hospitals and clinics throughout Liberia.

In every case, the hospitals were understaffed and lacking in many basic essentials and pharmaceuticals. This Ebola outbreak in Liberia has exposed the country's inherently weak health system. Less than 200 doctors existed in this country of 4 million prior to this epidemic. After the outbreak in March of this year, that number plummeted to only 50 doctors. This occurred as a result of the exodus of 95 percent of the expatriate doctors.

Prior to the Ebola outbreak, the nurses went on strike or slowed down work throughout the country due to work grievances. This was true in Lofa, Bong, Bomi, and Montserrado Counties, which have been hit hardest by the epidemic. These nurses returned to work after negotiations with the Ministry of Health just before Ebola entered the country. After the outbreak began claiming the lives of the nurses who did not have protective gear, the nurses fled the hospitals.

After a second Liberian doctor died of Ebola, all of the government hospitals shut down. The patients are too terrified to enter the buildings. The nurses have stated they will not return to work unless they are issued adequate protection including gloves, gowns, and goggles. At the ELW hospital in conjunction with Samaritans Purse, doctors and nurses continue to treat Ebola patients. There are 5 doctors and 77 nurses and aides. This is the only place in Monrovia where treatment for Ebola takes place. Currently, there is only enough space for 25 patients in the isolation center. Initial attempts to expand the unit were met with protests from the local community which did not want Ebola patients coming from all over Liberia into their community. Having allayed the fears of the community, Samaritan's Purse will complete an 80-bed unit in the next 2 weeks.

The only other treatment center in Liberia is a 40-bed unit in Lofa County. The case fatality rates range from 80 to 90 percent at both facilities, owing in part to the delays in people seeking treatment. Many patients die within 24 hours of presentation. ELWA is the only functioning hospital in Montserrado County, a population of nearly 1 million people where Monrovia is located. Many patients are dying with Ebola in their communities in part because there is simply no open health facilities.

This creates problems because whole families are getting infected and dying. There is no way to count all of the people dying of Ebola in the villages and in the remote areas. The cause of death is often unknown and there exists a lot of suspicion toward Western and government health workers. As a result, information is often withheld from health workers. Advice on safe burial practices or abstaining from eating bats and monkeys is oftentimes met with resistance and even violence against health workers.

To complicate matters further, usual illnesses such as malaria, typhoid, pneumonia, and surgical emergencies result in death as there are no functioning facilities at this time. The death toll will undoubtedly reach into the tens of thousands in Liberia unless immediate actions are taken to: 1) Increase the capacity to treat patients in isolation. 2) Create an effective means of quarantine for those suspected of having been exposed to Ebola. 3) Provide protective gear to all healthcare workers, and those involved in disposing of the bodies of patients that have expired.

Given the episodic nature of Ebola, we must begin investing in healthcare system strengthening as we prepare to deal with future outbreaks. SIM and SHIELD stand ready to assist in the building of capacity of west Africans by training and producing more African healthcare professionals. Thank you.

Mr. SMITH. Thank you so very much for your life-long commitment and for building up capacity and doing it yourself, and working with others at SIM.

[The prepared statement of Dr. Glover follows:]

Frank Eugene Glover, Jr., MD, DRPH, MPH, FACS
House Committee on Foreign Affairs
August 7, 2014
Combating the Ebola Threat

This Ebola outbreak in Liberia has exposed the country's inherently weak health system. Over the past few years I have spent three to four months per year in Liberia working in the health care sector. I have had the opportunity to visit most of the counties and tour the hospitals and medical establishments there. In every case the hospitals and clinics were understaffed and lacking in basic medical supplies and pharmaceuticals. Less than 200 doctors existed in this country of four million people prior to this epidemic. After the outbreak that number went down to about 50 doctors involved in clinical care. This occurred after the exodus of 95% of the expatriate doctors. To make matters worse, the nurses had not been paid in six months and were striking or "going slow" in counties throughout the country. This was true in Lofa, Bong, Bomi, and Montserrado counties which are the hardest hit by the Ebola outbreak. These nurses were convinced to return to work after negotiations with the Ministry of Health and Social Welfare in February of this year. After the outbreak began claiming the lives of the nurses, who did not have adequate protective gear, the nurses fled the hospitals. Once a couple of doctors died from Ebola, all of the government hospitals essentially closed. Patients refused to enter the buildings. The nurses have stated that they will only return to work if they receive adequate protection including gloves, gowns, and goggles.

At the ELWA hospital in conjunction with Samaritan's Purse, doctors continue to treat Ebola patients. There are five African doctors and 77 nurses and aides. This is the only place in Monrovia where treatment for Ebola can be obtained. There is only enough space for 25 patients. Attempts to expand the capacity to treat Ebola patients were resisted by the local community which feared having Ebola patients from around the country in their community. Protests began and health workers were assaulted. The case fatality rate is 80-90 percent owing in part to the delays in presenting for treatment. Everyday Ebola patients are turned away simply because the capacity has been exceeded. As a result of limited protective gear at ELWA the hospital emergency room has been shut down. Only obstetrical emergencies are handled currently.

Most patients are dying with Ebola in their communities because there is simply no where to go. This creates problems because whole families are getting sick and dying. There is no way to count all of the people dying in the villages and in remote areas. The cause of death is often unknown and there exists a lot of suspicion toward western and government health workers. As a result, information is often withheld from the health workers. Advice on safe burial practices and avoidance of eating bats and monkey meat oftentimes is met with hostility from those in the affected communities. Whole communities are being quarantined by police and military personnel. This inflames hostilities further.

Many dead bodies lie in the streets for days as the Ministry of Health does not have the capacity to dispose of all of the bodies in a timely manner. Those who are to dispose of the bodies complain that they are not being paid. During this rainy season the decomposition of the bodies and contamination of the environment becomes a concern. Communities are refusing to allow bodies to be buried in their communities fearing contamination of their water supply. There are reports of bodies being thrown into wetland areas as well as being partially buried in mass, shallow graves of up to 47 persons.

To complicate matters further, usual illnesses such as malaria, typhoid, pneumonia, and surgical illnesses result in death as there are no facilities functioning at this time due to the fear and lack of protective gear for health workers. I believe the death toll will reach the thousands in Liberia unless immediate action is taken to provide protective gear to the healthcare workers. Monrovia has a population of nearly a million people. Basic sanitation and potable water does not exist for most people living in this densely populated city. Given the episodic nature of Ebola, we must begin looking at healthcare system strengthening as we prepare to deal with future outbreaks. Education to produce African health professionals must be an essential part of this solution.

———

Mr. SMITH. Let me ask you a just a few questions because your testimonies I think were very comprehensive.

You said, Mr. Isaacs, that the international response you deemed it a failure and of course, no failure need be a failure in perpetuity. And I am wondering if there has been a turn of the corner; again, inspired by the tragedy of two of your workers being affected by the Ebola virus.

And secondly, could you tell us how are they doing; how are their spirits; whether or not there is a sense, even if it is not fully backed by science yet that the drug ZMapp may have had an impact? I think, you know, one of the things, one of the questions I asked of the earlier panel, if some of these interventions proved to be efficacious, delay is denial if you have Ebola and since this seems to be ramping up and not ramping down currently, your thoughts on an aggressive FDA working in cohort with and in conjunction with the other agencies of Government to get, based on an opt-in, certainly recognizing the risks as Dr. Brantly certainly did, and Ms. Writebol?

Mr. ISAACS. So on the failure aspect, I would say that I think the full international impact of Ebola has not been realized. I believe that Ebola threatens the stability of the three countries where it is effected right now. My staff met with the President of Liberia for almost 6 hours last Wednesday. They described to me that the atmosphere in the room was somber because she realized the full gravity of it.

If you read the Ministry of Health status reports that come out every day from Liberia, I don't mean to be dramatic, but it has an atmosphere of "Apocalypse Now" in it. There are bodies lying in the street. It is on the front page of the Wall Street Journal, and today, there are gangs threatening to burn down hospitals, and this is essentially a society that is, let us say, a generation from everybody had Posttraumatic Stress Disorder from a horrible war. They can go from a normal conversation to a fistfight, to sticks in the flash of an eye. So they have a lot of temperament and they have a lot of investment in what is going on. There is a lot of emotion. But it isn't just Liberia. It is Sierra Leone, it is all of these countries.

What would happen, you know, I don't want to, I mean, you can use your own imagination in Nigeria, Lagos, what could happen there? And I believe that this disease has the potential to be a national security risk for many nations. And I think it will have an impact even on our national security. It has been a failure because it is now jumped another country because the epidemiologists have totally misread the magnitude of the disease and because there are not resources on the ground.

The status of the two patients, I can say that I hear from Emory the same thing everybody does. They seem to be getting a little better every day. I do not think this will be a fast process. After that medicine was administered, after it was brought to us by the NIH people, and Dr. Brantly was very much involved in giving his informed consent to it. He understood as did Nancy Writebol. There was improvement, and I think as the doctors were saying here, I am not a doctor, you know, I don't want to guess at science, but I will say that they seem to have gotten better. They got home, they are at Emory. We appreciate Emory, they are getting good treatment there and we just pray that they survive and can recover their health.

Mr. SMITH. Let me ask you, you pointed out four different areas: Kissing the corpse, community health workers, medical professionals, as three of those.

Now let me ask you about the community health workers. You have pointed out that in one cluster of infected individuals 8 out of 12 were community health workers. Now, doctors obviously have a higher degree of training, they understand the essential importance of protective garb, and community health workers might not have that same level of indoctrination about how important that is.

In your view, are they much more at risk because they are more rudimentary in what they do and therefore they are not taking the precautions?

Mr. ISAACS. So in my view, yes, they are more at risk. It is not just to do with the personal protective gear, but it is also due to the lack of education. If you look at the symptoms of the disease, fever, joint pain, vomiting, and diarrhea, I am going to guess that probably covers 50 percent of all the diseases that present to them. That puts them in an untenable and weak position of being exposed to the disease, and not exactly knowing what it is.

I just am saying that I think that there needs to be focused education efforts on these four levels of society: General public awareness, community health workers, medical professional, and national leaders. I don't think putting a poster up on the wall saying ''Ebola kills'' is going to do it. I think that there has to be a programmatic approach to each one of these stratums of society to get the essential information that they need to encourage people from their position and to deal with the things that come to them.

Mr. SMITH. Doctor, please.

Dr. GLOVER. I would have a slightly different take on it. I believe that community health workers, if properly trained, can get the same outcome of coverage as physicians. What we have to understand is that people, health workers, don't get Ebola because of carelessness, necessarily, or because of lapses in sterile technique.

In the case of these workers, for example, it is very likely that they contracted Ebola from other workers who were at the hospital who may have gotten the disease from the community. So if you are working alongside someone and they happen to have Ebola, then you get it from the staff and so there are a number of documented cases of staff infecting staff. In fact, just yesterday there was a report in the Kakata, in Margibi County where four nurses died and 11 more were infected. And so there is a lot about the infectivity that we don't realize in terms of how it happens.

Mr. SMITH. Let me just, in terms of getting the message out in a way that will be most likely received so that people understand the catastrophic nature of the disease, my understanding is that Guinea today is recruiting retired doctors, nurses, and midwives, authority figures, older rather than younger, to convey this message.

Have you heard that and are the other countries, the other two countries and perhaps even Nigeria, too, looking to do that so that authority figures convey, again, the paramount importance of, for example, burial practices and the like?

Dr. GLOVER. One of the challenges we have in Liberia is after this 14-year brutal civil war, during that period of time people did not go to school. So you have a large population of illiterate people and many of the languages in Liberia are not scripted, so you can't write something. So there needs to be language-appropriate messaging in each dialect in a way that each community can understand it, so they can get the message.

So it requires people that are seen as authority figures, but also people that are able to communicate in the person's spoken language so they are able to get the message. So as he says, putting a poster up is not going to help someone when you have got an illiteracy rate of 75 percent.

Mr. SMITH. Finally, just let me ask, Mr. Isaacs, if you could, you said that the President of Liberia was a month late. Is it too late? And what would have happened had that state of emergency been declared a month ago?

Mr. ISAACS. The month statement was not a scientific statement. It is just an opinionated statement, and when I don't have knowledge, I always have opinions, rightly or wrongly. But I do think that Liberia would have been better served had a status of emergency been declared earlier.

Now, I don't know all of the actual mechanisms that will go along with that declaration, but it is clear to me that Liberia is in a severe crisis that I believe threatens the stability of the society as it exists today and I think that as you see the disease spread in Freetown and in Conakry, hopefully it has peaked there, and in Monrovia you are going to see more instability and insecurity.

Mr. SMITH. Then we do ask about the question of testing and you heard the exchange earlier with Dr. Frieden and other members of the panel about the lack of labs, lack of testing capability. You might want to comment on that. But even in the best of circumstances, say in New York, or New Jersey, how long does it take to get a test back? Because this does move very fast.

Dr. GLOVER. Well, we have special tests in the U.S. so in just a matter of a few hours.

Mr. SMITH. Hours.

Dr. GLOVER. But logistically, when you look at the infrastructure of these countries, to go from one point to the other on a map, it may look like, "Oh, it is just 50 miles." That 50 miles could take you 8 hours because you can only drive 3 miles an hour through roads that are impassable.

So a lot of logistical problems exist here, but I believe the number one cause of healthcare worker infections in Liberia is the lack of the protective gear. You are asking people to go to work, to take care of patients, and they don't have simple gloves. And to me this is unconscionable. So if we are going to put people on the line, the brightest and the best people in the country on the line, we owe it to them to give them a fighting chance.

Even in this country, no matter how well-trained a doctor is, if an Ebola patient comes up to him before he or she knows what he has, he has already been infected.

Mr. SMITH. Mr. Isaacs, you asked the question earlier, where will the money go? What will it buy? Where in your opinion should the money go and what should it buy?

Mr. ISAACS. I think that international personnel are needed. I frankly do not think that the Ministry of Health of Liberia can fight this. They do not have the case investigation capacity. I talked with a senior person in CDC, I won't name her, but she is a well-known person. She told me that in the United States if there was one person that had a Level 4 infectious disease, they would have many hundreds of contacts to run down. There are no contacts being run down in Liberia.

I don't believe that the Liberian Government, as well intentioned as they are, and I do believe that they are well intentioned, I just do not think that they have the capacity. I am all for building the capacity, but I think there needs to be something to augment their capacity. I think that there needs to be some kind of a coordination unit. I have heard here today that the World Health Organization has the lead; maybe, maybe not. I think that probably something perhaps with a bit more of an operational edge to it is called for. I don't know what that could be, but more is needed.

And I think that if we leave this situation up to the Ministries of Health, I mean, you have a unique situation where you have three poor countries that have a communicable, infectious, and lethal disease, that clearly don't have the capacity to contain it, and is the world willing to allow the public health of the world to be in their hands while they try to contain the disease? I think that is the essential question.

Mr. SMITH. Thank you. And finally, Dr. Glover, you had worked on the DRC outbreak of Ebola, what, some 20 years ago?

Dr. GLOVER. Actually, I was, at that time I was working in Zaire. I was in Zaire, in Kinshasa, but the outbreak was in Kikwit, so I was there during the outbreak, but I wasn't actually working with Ebola.

Mr. SMITH. How does this compare to that outbreak?

Dr. GLOVER. There is no comparison because back then it was a very sparsely populated rural area, where it could essentially burn itself out.

But you have so many people in Liberia that have moved to the city, so that they are living in very close spaces—if you look at a taxicab or a bus, you wonder how could they get so many people jam packed in there or how many people live in a house, for example. At the Phebe Hospital, the administrator came down with the virus, and he infected his 8 children, and his wife and all 10 of them died.

So the close proximity in which the people are living, the concentration of the population, means that as this epidemic, no matter what we do, unfortunately, there is going to be tremendous loss of life just by the nature of this disease.

Mr. SMITH. Well, I thank you both.

Is there anything you would like to add before we conclude the hearing?

Mr. ISAACS. I would just say that I think much more—I am certain there is much more than I know of, but this concept of research and development for a vaccine and a cure is very important. I agree with Dr. Glover. I think we are going to see death tolls in numbers that we can't imagine right now. That is potential and also, I will tell you that we are now at Samaritan's Purse in the process of distributing Ebola-readiness information to all missionary hospitals across Africa.

Mr. SMITH. Dr. Glover, any final words?

Dr. GLOVER. No final words.

Mr. SMITH. Thank you.

I want to thank both of you, again, for your extraordinary service to mankind and especially to the sick, and at risk, and disabled, and those who are suffering this terrible outbreak of Ebola.

And we look forward if you could stay in touch with our subcommittee, this is the first of a series of hearings. We are looking to make sure that whatever we need to do as a Congress, and as a subcommittee, and me personally, and my colleagues, we want to do and again, your guidance is absolutely essential.

Thank you for sharing your wisdom and insights, and incisive commentary to the subcommittee. The hearing is adjourned.

Mr. ISAACS. Thank you.

Dr. GLOVER. Thank you.

[Whereupon, at 4:23 p.m., the subcommittee was adjourned.]

APPENDIX

MATERIAL SUBMITTED FOR THE RECORD

SUBCOMMITTEE HEARING NOTICE
COMMITTEE ON FOREIGN AFFAIRS
U.S. HOUSE OF REPRESENTATIVES
WASHINGTON, DC 20515-6128

Subcommittee on Africa, Global Health, Global Human Rights, and International Organizations
Christopher H. Smith (R-NJ), Chairman

August 7, 2014

TO: MEMBERS OF THE COMMITTEE ON FOREIGN AFFAIRS

You are respectfully requested to attend an OPEN hearing of the Committee on Foreign Affairs, to be held by the Subcommittee on Africa, Global Health, Global Human Rights, and International Organizations in Room 2172 of the Rayburn House Office Building (and available live on the Committee website at www.foreignaffairs.house.gov):

DATE: Thursday, August 7, 2014

TIME: 2:00 p.m.

SUBJECT: Combating the Ebola Threat

WITNESSES: Panel I
Tom Frieden, M.D.
Director
Centers for Disease Control and Prevention

Ariel Pablos-Méndez, M.D.
Assistant Administrator
Bureau for Global Health
U.S. Agency for International Development

The Honorable Bisa Williams
Deputy Assistant Secretary
Bureau of African Affairs
U.S. Department of State

Panel II
Mr. Ken Isaacs
Vice President of Program and Government Relations
Samaritan's Purse

Frank Glover, M.D.
Missionary
SIM

By Direction of the Chairman

COMMITTEE ON FOREIGN AFFAIRS

MINUTES OF SUBCOMMITTEE ON _Africa, Global Health, Global Human Rights, and International Organizations_ HEARING

Day____*Thursday*____Date____*August 7, 2014*____Room_*2172 Rayburn HOB*_

Starting Time____*2:00 p.m.*____Ending Time ___*4:24 p.m.*___

Recesses |__*0*__| (____to ____)(____to ____)(____to ____)(____to ____)(____to____)(____to ____)

Presiding Member(s)

Rep. Chris Smith

Check all of the following that apply:

Open Session ☑   Electronically Recorded (taped) ☑
Executive (closed) Session ☐   Stenographic Record ☑
Televised ☑

TITLE OF HEARING:

Combating the Ebola Threat

SUBCOMMITTEE MEMBERS PRESENT:

Rep. Karen Bass

NON-SUBCOMMITTEE MEMBERS PRESENT: _(Mark with an * if they are not members of full committee.)_

Rep. Frank Wolf*

HEARING WITNESSES: Same as meeting notice attached? Yes ☑ No ☐
(If "no", please list below and include title, agency, department, or organization.)

STATEMENTS FOR THE RECORD: _(List any statements submitted for the record.)_

Statement for the record of Rep. Ed Royce

TIME SCHEDULED TO RECONVENE _____
or
TIME ADJOURNED ___*4:24 p.m.*___

Gregory B Simpkins
Subcommittee Staff Director

Questions for the Record Submitted to
Deputy Assistant Secretary Bisa Williams by
Representative Frank Wolf (#1 - #4)
Subcommittee on Africa, Global Health, Global Human Rights, and International
Organizations,
House Committee on Foreign Affairs
August 7, 2014

Question (1):

Ambassador Williams, over the years, we have heard from ambassadors and embassy staff that Washington does not take cables from them seriously. When did the State Department in the District of Columbia in Washington here first get a cable notification from the embassies of Sierra Leone, Guinea and Liberia about the Ebola crisis?

Answer:

The U.S. Embassy in Conakry reported the first suspected cases of the Ebola virus disease to the State Department on March 22, 2014 and convened its first Emergency Action Committee on the same day. A reporting cable followed on March 24, 2014, which was followed by a consistent stream of reporting messages and cables in the following weeks and months. U.S. embassies in the neighboring capitals, especially Monrovia and Freetown, sent out regular cables reporting on the preparatory steps the embassies and host governments were taking in response to the outbreak in Guinea. On April 1, 2014, the U.S. Embassy in Monrovia sent its first reporting cable on the possible spread of the disease from Lofa County in Liberia to Montserrat County where the capital is located. The Department received the first cable reporting a confirmed Ebola case in Freetown on May 27, 2014. The sequencing and intensity of these reports reflected the progression of the disease.

Question (2):

It is often we hear -- and, as you know, my district in northern Virginia, we have many. And they say that sometimes the cable gets sent and they wonder if -- so I would like to know when the cables were sent. And, secondly, how high in the State Department were the concerns raised, at what level and what time?

Answer:

Upon receiving the first cable from Guinea, the Department immediately notified the Centers for Disease Control and Prevention (CDC) and requested assistance. CDC deployed an additional five experts to join their personnel already stationed in the affected regions of Guinea on March 31 to assist with surveillance, contact tracing, and other response measures, and has since repeatedly surged staff to the affected countries to assist with response efforts. From the very beginning of the outbreak, high level officials in the Department and other agencies were briefed and regularly updated on the affected missions' actions to assist host governments to respond appropriately to the outbreak.

As you have heard in testimony from my colleagues from CDC and USAID, initial response efforts from local health providers, CDC personnel, aid workers, and World Health Organization (WHO) technical experts seemed to slow the outbreak for a time. During this time, our efforts were commensurate with the level of the outbreak. We continued to work with our missions in the affected countries as they mounted messaging campaigns to educate local populations and encouraged national governments to increase response and preparation efforts. By June 2014, when it was apparent that the virus was not contained, and was a greater danger to the urban populations in the region, we ramped up our response, intensifying our interagency coordination to identify the needs on the ground and how best to fill them. Through USAID and DoD, we provided technical assistance, and in-kind assistance, including gloves, masks, and personal protective equipment. At the working level, and at higher levels, we reached out to our partners to galvanize their assistance efforts. Assistant Secretary for African Affairs Linda Thomas-Greenfield, Undersecretary for Political Affairs Sherman, and Deputy Secretary Heather Higginbottom, all reached out to their counterparts in Europe as well as the affected countries to urge increased assistance and offer U.S. support as needed. In large part due to our mobilization efforts to raise awareness of the seriousness of this crisis, we have seen in recent months more resources brought to bear in the response efforts from the WHO, as well as our partners around the world.

Question (3):

You mentioned the work in response of USAID and State and others. What other donor nations have gotten involved in the efforts? And what exactly are they doing? Can you give us a list of the countries? You said, Dr. Frieden, you have 40 to 50 people coming. Can you tell us what the United Kingdom and France are doing and give us some specification as to numbers and how they are cooperating. Because we are -- it all cannot be the United States. What are our European allies and others doing, in numbers, if you can?

Answer:

As of August 7, the date of this hearing, the WHO is leading the international assistance efforts and in addition to providing direct assistance through cash and in-kind contributions, we are also reaching out to our international partners to provide similar support to the WHO. Like us, several of our international partners have been engaged in response efforts since the first wave of the outbreak begun in March 2014. For example, French research institutes – in particular INSERM (French National Institute of Health and Medical Research) and the Institut Pasteur – identified the outbreak of the epidemic and have been actively helping ever since to diagnose and monitor the disease. Several French experts are present on the ground to support the care of patients, the control of the epidemic and the training of staff, alongside local, French and international non-governmental organizations (NGOs), particularly Médecins Sans Frontières.

Since the second wave of the outbreak begun in June until August 7, we have been galvanizing support from our partners in Europe and the WHO to surge efforts to contain the virus. The Department of State and USAID are actively working with key donor countries, including the United Kingdom, France, Germany, and Norway, as well as the European Commission, to coordinate assistance and provide political leadership in support of the WHO and UN response plans. All of these partners share our assessment of how serious the situation has become, and like the United States are gearing up to provide increasing assistance as the response begins running more smoothly and effectively. In Geneva, our Mission is participating in an Ambassadorial-level "Contact Group" started by the UK that includes the affected nations and provides assistance coordination and strategic-level advice to the WHO.

Question (4):

Are the Chinese involved, who have historically invested in soccer stadiums in Africa? Are they involved? Is the Chinese Government that has invested in soccer stadiums in Africa -- are they involved, the Chinese Government?

Answer:

As of August 7, China has reportedly contributed $20,000 to the Liberian Red Cross Society to fight Ebola. We do not have any additional information about China's cash and/or in-kind contributions to the response efforts.

Opening Statement of the Honorable Ed Royce (R-CA), Chairman
House Foreign Affairs Committee
Subcommittee on Africa, Global Health, Global Human Rights, and International
Organizations Hearing on
"Combating the Ebola Threat"
August 7, 2014

(Submitted for the Record)

I want to thank Chairman Smith for convening this hearing, which will address ongoing efforts to track, contain, and combat Ebola. The House is not in session this week, but given the extraordinary circumstances of the outbreak in West Africa, this hearing is absolutely warranted.

As our witnesses will attest, Ebola is a rare but deadly communicable disease. Prior outbreaks occurred mainly in Central Africa and, while tragic, were relatively brief and limited in scale.

That is what makes this outbreak in West Africa so alarming. Whereas 425 people reportedly were infected and 224 people died during the 2000-2001 outbreak in Uganda, over 1,600 cases and nearly 900 deaths have been reported in West Africa. It has been six months since the first case was detected, and the rate of new infections appears to be accelerating. Stigma and fear are making it difficult to trace transmission. Moreover, the communities being impacted are highly mobile. As a result, we are seeing cases of transmission in Lagos, Nigeria and, perhaps, as far as Saudi Arabia.

According to the director-general of the World Health Organization (WHO), Margaret Chan, "If the situation continues to deteriorate, the consequences can be catastrophic in terms of lost lives but also severe socioeconomic disruption and a high risk of spread to other countries." Clearly, Ebola presents a transnational threat that must be urgently addressed.

What is different about this outbreak? Why is it so virulent? Has there been a change in the epidemiology of the virus? If not, is it spreading because affected communities don't have the necessary information or capacity to deal with it? If it is a capacity issue, what can the international community do to help? What measures have the governments of Guinea, Liberia, and Sierra Leone put in place to contain the outbreak? What more could they do? What is the role of the World Health Organization, donors, and the United States Government? Is there a role to be played by experts from Central Africa who have experience in dealing with Ebola? And how can we better communicate so that people can get the information they need to help detect, contain, and deter infections while avoiding mass panic?

On this last point, I also would like to get better clarity on how the Embassies are communicating with American citizens in Liberia, Guinea, and Sierra Leone. Have warden messages been sent out? Are the Embassies being responsive to inquiries and requests for assistance?

I have spoken directly to President Ellen Johnson Sirleaf, who is appealing to the United States to stand by our regional friend and ally in this time of crisis. I have assured her that we will. We also stand by the selfless health professionals and humanitarians who are responding to the outbreak. We will hear today from two organizations that have been on the front lines. Each has paid a hefty price. They deserve our recognition and appreciation.

I was pleased by the announcement on Tuesday that the US Agency for International Development (USAID) and the Centers for Disease Control and Prevention (CDC) will soon make additional resources available, including the deployment of a Disaster Assistance Response Team to coordinate the U.S. Government response. This comes on top of the deployment of 50 technical experts from CDC to the region. I expect that the Economic Community of West African States, the African Union, the United Nations, and others will also step up to the plate to combat the Ebola threat.

I thank the witnesses for appearing today. I look forward to working with the Administration, our partners in West Africa, and international community to ensure that we are able to detect, deter, and contain the Ebola outbreak in West Africa, while simultaneously improving systems to prevent future outbreaks.

www.ingramcontent.com/pod-product-compliance
Lightning Source LLC
Chambersburg PA
CBHW080320290526
45790CB00005B/2125